WHERE GODS MAY DWELL

WHERE GODS MAY DWELL

Understanding the Human Condition

S. D. Gaede

Academie Books Grand Rapids, Michigan
Zondervan Publishing House

WHERE GODS MAY DWELL

Copyright © 1985 by The Zondervan Corporation
Grand Rapids, Michigan

ACADEMIE BOOKS
is an imprint of Zondervan Publishing House,
1415 Lake Drive S.E., Grand Rapids, Michigan 49506

Library of Congress Cataloging in Publication Data

Gaede, S. D.
    Where Gods may dwell.

        Bibliography: p.
        1. Sociology, Christian.   2. Religion and science—1946-   .   I. Title.

BT738.G33   1985   261.5   85–11853

ISBN 0–310–42971–4

Edited by Kathryn Long and Ed van der Maas

Designed by Louise Bauer

Printed in the United States of America

85   86   87   88   89   90   91   92 / 11   10   9   8   7   6   5   4   3   2   1

For the structure that we raise,
    Time is with materials filled;
Our todays and yesterdays
    Are the blocks with which we build.

Truly shape and fashion these;
    Leave no yawning gaps between;
Think not, because no man sees,
    Such things will remain unseen.

In the elder days of Art,
    Builders wrought with greatest care
Each minute and unseen part;
    For the gods see everywhere.

Let us do our work as well,
    Both the unseen and the seen;
Make the house where gods may dwell
    Beautiful, entire, and clean.

Henry Wadsworth Longfellow,
"The Builders"

CONTENTS

PREFACE

At some point during graduate school, it became abundantly clear to me that the personal predispositions of a scholar affect his or her scholarly output. In my own field of sociology, for example, where most scholars confess a desire to produce a wholly "objective" product, I discovered that the fruit tasted differently depending upon the soil in which the analysis was rooted. This observation, which I later learned was far from original, was the progenitor of my present interest in Christian thinking about the social or human sciences.

During my years as an undergraduate sociology major, I was introduced to a wide range of social science literature. This reading convinced me of two things: one, that significant conflicts existed between aspects of my Christian faith and the writings of many social scientists; and two, that these same social scientists nevertheless appeared to be saying some important and exciting things. Their analyses could not simply be dismissed as erroneous. I made some superficial attempts as an undergraduate to resolve this inherent conflict, but by and large I lived with a roaring internal debate.

In graduate school, particularly during my years at Vanderbilt, I decided to pursue two areas that seemed to generate the greatest degree of internal conflict: sociology of religion and social stratification. Though I took my comprehensive exams in the latter, the former seemed to create the most inner tension, and so (being a latent masochist) it became the focus of my dissertation and later research. Social stratification, though provocative because of the significant Marxist influence in the field, was for that same reason less ambiguous. It was far easier to specify the issues and to resolve the inherent conflict there— or so I thought. In the sociology of religion, however, there was a long tradition of "objective" scholarship arriving at "scientific" conclusions that seemed to blatantly contradict my own Christian world view. This, I decided, was where I would stake my sociological future.

As I pursued the sociology of religion, I became intent on resolving this internal struggle. Something was wrong either with my faith or with my science; they could coexist no longer in their present form. Since I was rationally and emotionally committed to both of them, however, I was determined not to let either truth claim slip away easily. I was not about to terminate my commitment to either perspective on the basis of one or two cheap shots. I wanted to see demonstrated error.

This determination had an interesting effect on my intellectual adventure; it forced me to ask irreverent questions, not only about my faith but also about the conclusions reached by the social scientist. That process eventually unearthed a whole host of hidden assumptions about the nature of and methodology within the social sciences. Among other things, I learned that these covert assumptions (1) greatly delimited the social science task; (2) were arbitrary and by their nature required faith; and (3) were by no means essential to scientific investigation. Indeed, after playing with alternative assumptions, I found that one could arrive at significantly different scientific conclusions from the same set of empirical observations.

Though this discovery was a gradual one, its personal impact was substantial. On the one hand, I was frustrated that an issue of this magnitude could for so long go unnoticed, not only by myself, but also by many within the social science community. On the other hand, I was elated to learn that the conflicts between my science and my Christianity were neither inherent nor endemic. I also came away with the conviction that I could no longer engage in naive social science, unconcerned about the presuppositional base of the scientist. There was work to do, and it lay at the level of the assumptions that undergird modern scientific thought. This book is a part of that effort.

*   *   *
**   **   **

What you hold in your hand, therefore, is first of all an attempt to explain the need for Christian thinking in the social sciences and secondly an effort to ruminate upon and work toward the development of such thinking. The first issue is important because there are many within the scientific community who would doubt the need for, or the legitimacy of, Christian thinking in the social sciences. Their incredulity, moreover, is well grounded since it is supported by the bulk of scientific thought in the twentieth century. Thus, it is essential to begin our discussion with the question, Why? Why bother to think Christianly about the social sciences? What is the need? Do we have the right to do so?

But once we are convinced that the project is worth doing, we are still left with the question of *how* it should be done. How should we engage in Christian social science anyway? It is one thing to think that it should be done; it may be quite another to actually pull it off! To shed some light on this issue, I have attempted in the second part of this book to apply Christian assumptions about the scientific task to the topic of human relationships. I choose this topic because it is a familiar one in the social sciences and because I think it is crucial to an adequate understanding of the human condition.

I would be less than candid, however, if I failed to confess that this task is being undertaken with more than a modicum of misgiving. I am concerned that more will be expected of this book than can be offered at this time. Therefore, let me try to make clear what this book is not and makes no attempt to be.

First and foremost, this is not "the" Christian approach to the study of human relationships. In my opinion, "the" Christian approach to human relationships cannot be written by fallible human beings—and certainly not by me. Moreover, one always hopes that newer and better attempts will come along in the future to antiquate previous efforts. I am confident that such will be the case here.

Second, I have not sought to construct an in-depth analysis and critique of the social sciences. Rather, I have attempted to hone in on those issues that seem most salient and crucial, either as an impediment to or as a springboard for a Christian understanding of human relationships. I realize that in doing this I run the risk of making my analysis appear underdeveloped; and in some ways, that is a fair critique. I trust it does not seem superficial as well.

Finally, because this book takes the form of an argument rather than a text, and because its audience includes both the interested layperson and the scientist, I have departed somewhat from the parameters of standard scientific scholarship. My first priority has been communication: to present my thoughts in a readable style. I have used footnotes sparingly—only to guide the reader to relevant literature or to explain a potentially troublesome statement. Though this may not be an appropriate format for the majority of scholarly endeavors, it seems the most suitable in this case, considering my objectives and the purposes of the book.

Returning to what this book is, rather than what it is not, I would suggest that it is an invitation—an invitation to taste the fruit of a social science built on Christian assumptions regarding the form and substance of ultimate reality. The invitation is offered to all who have an interest in the relationship between thought and faith, to all for whom the future of Christian scholarship is more than a passing fancy. Thus, the audience is not limited by area of expertise but by degree of curiosity.

Above all, this book is a personal statement—one individual's attempt to gain a Christian understanding of the human condition and to apply that understanding, without apology, to the world of the social sciences.

ACKNOWLEDGMENTS

In writing this book, I incurred a great debt to members of the Gordon College community. The ideas presented here, though free-floating for a time, took root in Gordon soil, were nurtured and pruned by Gordon minds, and were harvested by dint of a Gordon sabbatical. Needless to say, this does not mean that Gordon scholars are the least bit culpable for any mutations that may appear.

Two people deserve special thanks: Robert A. Clark, for the breadth of his expertise and the depth of his Christian wisdom—and his generosity with both; and Judy Lynn Gaede, for the intrepid judgments of her editorial eye and the undaunted prejudices of her ever-loving heart.

WHERE GODS MAY DWELL

THINKING CHRISTIANLY ABOUT THE SOCIAL SCIENCES:

A QUESTION OF ASSUMPTIONS

If our exploration is to have any significance at all, we must first answer an important question: What need do we have of "Christian" thinking—in the social sciences or anywhere else?

In the tradition of Alvin Gouldner,[1] I am tempted to begin my argument with a number of disparaging remarks about the state of modern scholarship. By convincing you that the "Halls of Ivy" are riddled with termites and rotten at the core, I might be able to set the stage for a Christian alternative. I will not take that approach, however. Not that I am above it, to be sure. As the reader will discover, I am more than willing to take a pot shot now and then, especially when the target is large and relatively exposed. But a credible argument must start at the beginning, and the malignancies of modern academics did not spawn my present interest in Christian scholarship.

Instead, I will initiate this discussion with one pertinent fact: I am a Christian. This is a reality of no small importance to me. It has implications for my thoughts, my actions, my entire life. Scholarship is a part of my life. As my Christianity makes a difference in how I act (or should act), it also makes a difference in how I think (or should think). If one's faith is important enough to encompass the personal life, then I see no reason to neglect its application to the rest of life as well. In my opinion, I am just as obligated to be concerned with a Christian perspective in my scholarly pursuits as I am in matters pertaining to ethics, family life, or whatever.

The point, of course, is that Christians should allow their Christianity to permeate their entire lives and not just preselected segments of it. To me, there is something terribly obvious about this point. It is the kind of truth one wants to label "fundamental" or "basic."

And yet there are certain problems associated with it. For one thing, experience tells me that it is not a very persuasive line of reasoning with some Christians, particularly those in the modern college or university. Many Christian scholars, for example, will feel that my argument is simplistic and ignores the need for scholastic objectivity. Others may say that it relates only tangentially to non-Christians: Even if non-Christians agree, for example, that life should be lived in some consistent fashion, why should they be interested in a Christian perspective on human relationships? After all, they disagree with its philosophical base. Moreover, many scholars, both Christian and non-Christian, believe that "scholarship is scholarship," regardless of a person's philosophy of life. For them, the idea of Christian—or Marxist or humanistic—scholarship makes very little sense because it makes very little difference.

There is, then, a variety of responses to the possibility of or need for Christian scholarship. One group seems to think it is wrong; another group feels it is irrelevant; and the third is convinced that it is inconsequential. And yet there is a common, underlying thread weaving its way through each of the above criticisms. What these responses have in common relates not only to the scholar but to people in all walks of life. It is the question of assumptions.

Stated simply, the question is, How do assumptions affect the way we think and the actions we take? On this question, I suspect, turns the entire issue of the legitimacy, possibility, and need for Christian scholarship. For this reason, the question of assumptions is the focus of the next six chapters. Chapter 1 discusses the question in general terms and is an attempt to see the relevance of assumptions for our personal lives as well as for the professional life of the scientist. Chapter 2 questions the source and interrelatedness of assumptions. Chapter 3 considers the connection between Christian assumptions and the early development of Western (or modern) science, a question that is pursued further in chapter 4 where it helps us answer another question: What is the source of the assumptions of twentieth-century science? Chapter 5 examines the state of contemporary science and explores the problematic effects of its assumptions. Finally, in chapter 6, we will direct our attention specifically to the social sciences and ask about their health and general well-being.

Such questions, I believe, will not only lead us to a better understanding of the relevance of assumptions in science, but set the stage as well for the development of a Christian social science perspective in part B. Though these questions may appear somewhat esoteric or abstruse, in truth they are neither. Without them, our thinking will be less clear, not more; with them, we may begin to discern the nature of the modern scientific enterprise. For those whose interest is in truth, nothing could be more practical—or more important.

Chapter 1

ASSUMPTIONS AND SCIENCE: EVER THE TWAIN SHALL MEET

If it were possible to "do" one's thinking in a vacuum, free of all assumptions, preconceptions, and evaluations, then maybe there would be little need for Christian scholarship. Indeed, most arguments for value-free scholarship assume that doing such a thing is possible. In fact, however, neither scholarship nor any other human activity is untouched by assumptions. Nature abhors a vacuum. Where assumptions exist, they affect our behavior; where they do not exist, we fabricate them in order to rationalize our actions. To put this fundamental truth differently, if we do not approach scholarship on the basis of Christian assumptions about the nature of reality, then we are getting our assumptions somewhere else. In chapter 2 we will look at the sources of these assumptions. But first we need to consider the question of assumptions and how they affect us.

A MIDNIGHT RIDE

I remember an incident that occurred when I was a teenager. I went out with friends one evening and lost track of the time. Sooner than I realized, the wee hours of the morning had arrived and I was in a hurry to get to my parents' home.

As usually happens in such situations, my attempt was thwarted by one obstacle after another. First there was the proverbial truck on a two-lane road, the kind that blocks your vision, vacillates between forty-five and eighty-five miles per hour, and emanates odors of dubious salubrity. Whenever the truck went slowly, I was unable to pass, either because of oncoming traffic or because road signs would not permit it. Whenever the path was clear, the truck would proceed with all the vigor of a cheetah on the chase.

Down the road I passed a car, sitting only partly on the shoulder, with its hood up and its emergency lights flashing. One or two miles past the car stood a man in a bow tie and tuxedo awkwardly attempting the art of hitchhiking. I felt that I should stop and help, but by now I was so anxious not to lose any more time that I drove by—thus adding guilt to my anxiety. Five or ten minutes beyond the hitchhiker I came upon a blinking yellow light attached to a sign that read "SLOW MEN AT WORK NEXT 5 MILES" (I have never been able to determine whether such signs make a demand of the driver or comment on the quality of the laborers), with a legal request to reduce my speed to twenty-five miles per hour. At 1:00 A.M., there were of course no men at work and not the least bit of evidence that anyone had worked on the road in the past century. Needless to say, I was wrought, distraught, waylaid, and dismayed.

In a sense, I think much of life is like that drive home. During the course of each day, we are confronted with a whole battery of decisions: What should we do about obstacles (like smelly trucks) that annoy us and impede our progress? How should we respond to people (like tuxedo-clad hitchhikers) who need our help but whose needs would cost us valuable time, money, or prestige? And what about all those rules that perpetually assault us—rules that don't always make sense but nevertheless demand obedience?

A thirty-minute slice of life is quite enough to reveal that we humans approach such decisions from diverse perspectives. Some of us choose risk, others safety; some choose to help, others to help themselves; some march in step, others to the beat of a different drummer.

In part this is because we don't all make the same assumptions about the nature of the world in which we live. We have different concepts of truth. Some people think laws are to be obeyed without exception; others believe that individual discernment is a prerequisite to lawful behavior; still others think that laws are to be used, or abused, for personal enjoyment. We behave differently because we make different assumptions—about law, about ethics, about the nature of humanity, or even about the reason for life itself.

ASSUMPTIONS IN SCIENCE

Many people would grant that assumptions played an important role in the above example; far fewer, however, will do so when we enter the realm of science. The reason, I think, has to do with the traditional image of science: a community of scholars objectively pursuing truth and reaching "scientific" conclusions with great regularity, consistency, and unanimity. It is often pointed out, for example, that although scientists come from a wide variety of backgrounds, holding different values, beliefs, and attitudes, they nevertheless reach remarkably similar conclusions when they enter their scientific laboratories. Thus, it is argued, assumptions seem to make very little difference in the task of scientific investigation.

Two points need to be made in response to this argument. First, it reflects a perspective on contemporary scientific activity that I am not sure is justified. In particular, it would be difficult to demonstrate that there is a high degree of uniformity or consistency among scientific claims—and certainly not the degree often assumed by outsiders. This is especially true in the human (or social) sciences, but I think it holds for the physical (or natural) sciences as well. The historical development of science, in particular, is liberally salted with contradictions, disagreements, and competing truth claims.[1]

Nevertheless, for the sake of discussion, let us assume that among a certain segment of scientists there is a great deal of unanimity relative to scientific methodology and conclusions. The question is, Does this *fact* demonstrate that assumptions do not play a significant role in the scientific arena? I would like to suggest that, if anything, it may demonstrate exactly the reverse—that at times assumptions can have a nearly determinative effect on behavior. Indeed, I would assert that to the extent that segments of the scientific community have been able to generate relatively consistent findings they have done so precisely because they have been able to reach a remarkable degree of consensus on the basic assumptions that undergird and guide their activity. That is, they have committed themselves to an explicit vision of how to go about finding scientific truth, what types of questions should be asked in the pursuit of scientific truth, and what kind of conclusions and interpretations are possible or impossible on the basis of this procedure. As we will see in the next section, all of these ideas are based upon *assumptions,* and these assumptions have a delimiting effect upon the investigative process. They serve to channel scientists in certain directions and prevent them from moving in others.

ASSUMPTIONS IN THE HUMAN SCIENCES

When we narrow our focus from science in general to the human sciences, we add to and complicate the question of assumptions common to all science by introducing the human being as the analytical focal point. Thus, Homo sapiens is not only the investigator, as in physical science, but also the "investigatee." This means that we are dealing not only with the assumptions, perceptions, and evaluations of the investigator, but also those of the subject—not to mention the highly complex interaction between the two.

The impact of assumptions on the human sciences can be observed in the works of Emile Durkheim, an early sociological theorist.[2] Durkheim is an interesting choice for our discussion because he was personally committed to the idea of an objective science, one that was free of all extraneous assumptions and which dealt only with the empirical facts. In spite of this perspective, or perhaps because of it, his painstaking research in the area of the sociology of religion led him to the rather stark and controversial conclusion that sacred objects as well as the gods are only a symbolic expression of society.[3]

Why did he come to this conclusion? First, Emile Durkheim was a naturalist. Reality for him was confined exclusively to the material world, which included the human phenomenon called religion. The relevant question for Durkheim, therefore, was, What natural phenomenon can explain the origin and development of religious expression? This question followed quite logically from his assumption that all observable phenomena result from natural causes. Second, on the basis of extensive studies exploring religious behavior among technologically primitive peoples, Durkheim concluded that a close relationship exists between the structure of society and religious sentiments. He meant that religious beliefs and rituals in a particular society seem to be directly related to the character of the society's social organization. Third, and finally, he theorized that societies develop religious symbols that express in concrete form the values and needs of a society. In other words, religious phenomena are the consequence of the social conditions within which they are found.

While many contemporary sociologists will agree that Durkheim's assumptions had a significant impact upon his sociological analysis, some will nevertheless claim that his analysis was the illegitimate product of "bad science." This raises the question, Were Durkheim's conclusions appropriate ones for a scientist to make? The question itself is interesting because it implies the existence of some set of universal criteria for judging what is and what is not "scientifically appropriate." Setting that rather dubious assumption aside, let me try to respond to the first question with another.

What is not scientifically appropriate about Durkheim's analysis? Certainly not his assumption that observable events have natural causes; few scientific discussions assume anything else. To the extent, therefore, that religion is an observable human phenomenon, it is available for understanding as a "natural" event. Nor can one find fault with his observation concerning the relationship between religious and social phenomena, whether or not one agrees with it or its implications. Such an observation seems to be well within the purview of science.

But is it legitimate for a sociologist to hypothesize that

human conceptions of God are mere projections of social reality? Should he have remained satisfied with the recognition of an "association" between the two rather than speculating about causal factors? As a journalist, maybe; as a sociologist, never. The notion of the causal influence of one variable on another is a cornerstone of most scientific theory; normally this is what is implied in the concept of "scientific explanation." To forbid Durkheim its use is tantamount to making him a sociological eunuch. No. I may not agree with his assumptions (and I do not), but I cannot condemn Durkheim for his line of reasoning. His only mistake was his tenacious application of the logic of his assumptions and his refusal to flinch when they took him into the heart of human affairs.

All of this leads us back to the central point of our discussion. The importance of Durkheim is not that he theorized about God or that he was a naturalist; his importance is that he shows quite clearly how assumptions channel sociological theorizing, leading to certain types of conclusions and not others. Furthermore, we have missed the point if we think this only occurs when we are theorizing about religion or discussing Emile Durkheim or sociology. Every sphere of human behavior is influenced by assumptions, from the most mundane activity to the highly touted and supposedly neutral enterprise of science.

IMPLICATIONS

If assumptions play such a significant role in science, then criticisms leveled at our argument for the need for Christian scholarship simply do not hold. The objective scientist, the unconcerned non-Christian, the indifferent scholar—each is refusing to deal with the reality of assumptions. And by acting as if assumptions are of little consequence, they are ignoring the very assumptions upon which they themselves are operating. Nothing could be more dangerous; it seems to me the surest route to intellectual folly.

And yet, they are not alone. Social science literature provides ample evidence to suggest that many scholars haven't the foggiest notion what their assumptions are or how they affect their scientific thinking.[4] While the reasons for this assumptive myopia are not entirely clear, its results certainly are. For the last fifty years professional journals have blindly paid homage to the gods of scientism, positivism, and empiricism.[5] It is my firm conviction that this kind of activity will continue indefinitely unless working scholars (1) begin to discover what their assumptions are; (2) attempt to settle questions about assumptions *before* they begin to construct their theories; and (3) make an effort to build their theories upon their chosen assumptions in a logically consistent fashion. For me, as a Christian scholar, this means that the first step toward the development of an adequate approach in the social sciences is the cultivation of a clear conception of the assumptions of a Christian world view.

Chapter 2

THE SOURCES OF ASSUMPTIONS: WORLD VIEWS

Statements about the ultimate nature of things are indicative of a person's world view. A world view may be defined as the totality of beliefs concerning the universe and the place and destiny of humanity within it, held by an individual, community, or society.[1] In general, a world view is that which a person believes to be true about reality. This would include, among other things, the individual's concept of God (His existence, nonexistence, and His nature), humanity, the universe, and the nature of morality. When people say that God is love, or that God is the product of human illusion, or that human beings are naturally egocentric, they are verbalizing portions of their world views.

The importance of world views is brought into clear relief when we ponder the basic points made in chapter 1: first, assumptions affect conclusions, in science as elsewhere; and second, *all* persons, with varying degrees of sophistication, hold assumptions concerning the ultimate nature of reality. This means that our world view, as a collective set of ultimate assumptions, plays a significant role in our life. It affects how we handle personal relationships, how we conduct ourselves in public and in private, how we use our spare time, and, of particular concern to us, how we go about engaging in scholarship.

Based on the definition of world view we have presented, it should be clear that an infinite variety of world views is possible. There are potentially as many world views as there are people. Furthermore, there is a great deal of ambiguity in the world views of most people, which adds to the complexity of the situation.

Regardless of this potential for complexity, the real world gives us a different picture. Despite the individuality that marks the lives of certain people, the norm in every society is conformity, not deviance, uniformity, not diversity.[2] However much each of us may wish to deny it, most of what we know and believe has been given to us by our parents, friends, community, and society. We learn more than we create; we accept more than we reject. In short, we do not develop our own private world views. At most, we refine and reconceptualize (normally the latter) what we have learned from others. It is the rare individual who carves his or her own unique philosophy of life; it is rarer still for society to praise that person's ingenuity and novelty. Such individuals are much more likely to be cast off as insane, dangerous, or both. And we, the peons of normalcy, find ourselves riddled with self-doubts and insecurity the moment we discover that we are not in lock step with the values of our culture.

This human tendency towards value conformity is important to our discussion of assumptions for two reasons. First, it means that for most of us our inherited world view constitutes the primary, though certainly not the only, source of our assumptions about the nature of reality. Second, it means that it is possible even in the most pluralistic of modern societies to specify the types of world views that tend to dominate the lives of any particular group of people. For example, in American society as well as in the West in general, three world views are probably more influential than any others—naturalism, pantheism, and theism.[3] More than many people realize, these world views and the assumptions each includes have had a profound impact on Western society—including science. Because of their importance for the question of assumptions, therefore, we will use the remainder of this chapter to explore these world views in greater depth.

NATURALISM

At its core, the naturalistic world view rests upon the belief that the material universe is the sum total of reality.[4] To put it negatively, naturalism holds to the proposition that the supernatural, in any form, does not exist. To Peggy Lee's melodic question "Is That All There Is?" the naturalist responds with a sincere yes. Naturalism is the philosophical manifestation of the once-popular phrase, "What you see is what you get."

The naturalistic world view assumes that the matter or stuff which makes up the universe has never been created but has always existed. This is because an act of creation presupposes the existence of some reality outside of, or larger than, the world order—incompatible with the tenet that the material universe is the sum total of reality. Naturalism normally assumes that always-existing matter has developed into the ordered universe which we see by a blind, timeless process of chance.[5] The human being, as one part of the natural universe, is also the result of matter, time, and chance. Within the context of the naturalistic world view, miracles, as such, do not exist; they are natural events which have yet to be explained.

Even a brief survey of social science literature will bear witness to the influence of the naturalistic world view within these disciplines.[6] For example, two important concepts within the social sciences—determinism and materialism—are basically derivatives of a naturalistic world view.

Determinism is the view that human choice is entirely controlled by previous conditions.[7] Thus, the history of humanity can be viewed as the result of conditioned responses to social, psychological, and other such stimuli. In my opinion, determinism takes two distinct forms within social science. The first is a kind of orthodox determinism which views human development in terms of an unbroken chain of cause and effect (e.g., strict Marxist or Skinnerian theory). The second type of determinism is usually more humanistic in tone and less inclined to embrace a particular explanatory model of development; it nevertheless assumes that human phenomena are the result of natural causes and are potentially explainable within a naturalistic framework. Closely allied with determinism is the concept of *materialism*. In its extreme form, material-ism assumes that nothing is real except matter itself.[8] Mind, consciousness, and thought patterns are all manifestations of matter and reducible to physical elements.

In general, I think it is safe to say that the naturalistic world view holds sway within the physical and human sciences today. Indeed, in most sectors of science the naturalistic world view is assumed, not debated. Few introductory texts in the human sciences, for example, even take the time to introduce the concept of world views or to delineate the assumptive context within which the authors operate. Nine times out of ten the authors of such texts assume—or take as normative for the discipline—the presuppositions of the naturalistic world view.

PANTHEISM

Despite the obvious dominance of the naturalistic world view, there are many today who believe that its influence is waning. They point to the rise of religious movements, the questioning of science and technology, and the despair of modern existentialism as evidence of its erosion. If they are correct, a partial explanation of this change would have to include a renewed interest in a pantheistic world view.

The belief that God is the sum total of reality and that the sum total of reality is God, may best exemplify the pantheistic world view.[9] The pantheist asserts that everything that exists constitutes a unity and that this all-inclusive unity is divine. For this reason the pantheist can say with great integrity that God is in everything—you, me, this book, your chair, everything. Probably one of the most difficult ideas for the materialistic mind-set to grasp is the pantheistic notion that physical reality does not exist—that the physical world is an illusion. (The pain of a stubbed toe, for example, is much too excruciating for the average Westerner to deny.)

Since pantheists assume that everything that exists consti-tutes one eternal reality, they also assume that there has never been a creation as such, although Hinduism is chock-full of creation stories. If all is one, then the concept of a Creator-God does not make much sense. Also, if there is only one reality

(God), the existence of the individual as an independent reality is an illusion. Similarly, within the pantheistic framework, miracles are not extraordinary events but are just as normal or ordinary as anything else. This follows logically from the pantheistic assumption concerning the illusory nature of the universe.

In general, the pantheistic world view has not been nearly as pervasive in the West as the naturalistic world view. This is especially true in the sciences, where matter and empirical reality seem to be the focus of attention. Nevertheless, within society in general there does seem to be a trend toward the wisdom of the East, most of which is permeated by a pantheistic world view. Among intellectuals, pantheism has for some time been a source of stimulation (e.g., Thoreau and Whitman), and some have predicted that its effect will be felt increasingly within the sciences,[10] especially in the disciplines of psychology and sociology.

THEISM

In direct contrast to the naturalists, theists begin their understanding of the nature of reality with God. Therefore, the most important question is, What are the characteristics of God? Within the Judeo-Christian tradition, the following assumptions are normally embraced. God is personal: He can be in relationship with other beings. God is eternal: He has always existed and will forevermore exist. God is infinite: He knows no limits and His being is immeasurable. God is perfect: His character is without flaw and His actions are free from error. God is transcendent: He is distinct from His creation. God is immanent: He is involved with and continually sustains the universe. God is love: He is the source of every good gift and the executor of all justice.

For the theist, the universe and all that exists came into being through the efforts of God, and God continues to sustain His creation. The latter point is important because it distinguishes most theists from deists. Deism emphasizes the transcendency of God and assumes that, although God created the world and the natural laws that govern it, He does not presently play an active role in the universe—the "watch-maker" concept of God. Most theistic traditions, however, assume that God is continually involved with His creation.

This creation, furthermore, is made up of both physical matter (the world of the naturalist) and nonmatter (the reality of the pantheist). Neither of these has always existed—both matter and finite spirit were created. Human beings, who have both a physical and a spiritual dimension, are a part of God's creation. They are unique, having been made in the image of God, and personal, their personality being grounded in the personality of God. Significantly for the theist, human beings are known by God personally and have the potential of being in relationship with God. Finally, given the characteristics of God, exceptional events, or miracles as they are called, are just as possible as ordinary or commonplace phenomena. That is because God is the author of both, the ever-present sustainer of regular patterns in nature and the ever-capable executor of exceptions to those regularities.

CONCLUSION: SOURCES OF WORLD VIEWS

In this chapter, I have attempted to present some of the basic postulates of three extremely influential world views, both because these world views are the source of many of our individual assumptions about the nature of reality and because, as we shall see, they have played a significant role in the development (or nondevelopment) of science.

Presenting these world views in such stark form, however, has one major disadvantage: It tends to give the impression that they can be understood apart from the major traditions which gave them birth. Such an impression would be most unfortunate. These world views did not simply arrive in their present form. Instead, they are the product of the historical development of a few influential world religions. Pantheism, for example, is the world view expressed in many of the great religions of the East, especially Hinduism. Theism, on the other hand, has its roots in the religion of the Hebrews; today it finds expression not only in Judaism but also in Islam and Christianity. The point, of course, is that humanity's religious inclinations are primarily responsible for the existence and present form of major world views.[11]

But what about naturalism? There appears to be nothing religious about this world view. How did it develop? With naturalism we have something of a different case, to be sure. Although it initially developed within the context of a specific religious tradition, it has come to be viewed as a nonreligious world view. In order to evaluate this claim, however, as well as to understand naturalism's evolution, we must first look at the development of science.

Chapter 3

THE IMPLICATIONS OF ASSUMPTIONS (1):

Christianity and the Origins of Modern Science

Understanding the historical development of modern science is not an easy task. Philosophers and historians of ideas have debated this topic for many years, at times with great tenacity and vehemence.[1] To suggest, therefore, that a mere sociologist with only modest exposure to the philosophy and history of science can provide even a modicum of insight into this matter is certainly questionable. Nevertheless, I am convinced that such insight is crucial to an adequate understanding of the relationship between assumptions and science. Thus, with flak jacket and parachute in place, we must take the leap that inevitably confronts us. I trust, however, that my readers will make every effort to corroborate the argument presented here with their own investigative adventure.

THE SACRED CANOPY OF SCIENCE

Modern science developed its peculiarly Western form during the sixteenth and seventeenth centuries. I am not as interested in the uniqueness of the type of science that developed as I am the philosophical framework within which it grew. In particular, is it possible to say that the rise of modern science took place within the context of a specific world view? I believe it is.

A great many scholars, both Christian and non-Christian, feel that modern science in its infancy was nourished at the breast of a Christian theistic world view.[2] This is not to deny or even take a position on the influence of other socio-ideological factors which may have been at play. Clearly there were many. Nor does this imply that Christianity is necessarily a precondition to all forms of science. Quite obviously that is not the case, since types of science have sprung up at various times in human history. It is merely to assert that Christianity was the sacred canopy within which modern science developed during sixteenth- and seventeenth-century Europe.

Of the many pieces of evidence that support this contention, one seems especially salient. Most of the major figures in the early development of modern science were Christians. This would include Copernicus, Galileo, Bacon, Kepler, and Newton. Storkey points out, for example, that "the earliest notable scientific group in France centering around Claude de Peiresc, Gassendi, Mersenne, Pascal," was made up of men who were "characterized by a strong Roman Catholic faith."[3] He argues as well, as does Robert Merton,[4] that the important early scientists in England were committed Christians, pointing to the works of Boyle, Ray, Gren, Oughtred, Barrow, Napier, and Newton to support his case. He says flatly that these men were not only zealous Christians and great scientists, but that "their faith motivated, shaped, and gave meaning to their science."[5]

The point is not that these seminal thinkers in science were influenced only by Christianity. No one, in any age, who lives on the exchange and development of ideas, is affected by only one philosophical or theological perspective. Some of these individuals, for example, grappled with—and at times tried to synthesize Christianity with—aspects of Greek thought. But these ideas were clearly not the primary context for their scientific thinking. That distinction seems to have been reserved for the Christian theistic world view.

Assuming the credibility of this thesis, why was Christian theism such a fertile world view for the growth and development of science? Again, this is a question that can be asked on many levels. For example, why did Christianity *at that particular point in time* produce certain effects? To find an answer, one would have to look not only at peculiar aspects of sixteenth-century Christianity, especially the dynamics of the Reformation and the Catholic reaction, but also at specific social developments in Europe. This is an interesting question and debate, but it is not what I want to address.

Rather, I would like to raise the question whether Christianity might offer a world view particularly favorable to the development of science. My thesis is that it does. This, I think comes into perspective when we compare certain key assumptions in Christian theism with those of pantheism.

CHRISTIAN ASSUMPTIONS AND THE DEVELOPMENT OF SCIENCE

In order for a community of scholars to engage in the systematic study of phenomena in this world, a number of elements must be present. The most obvious of these is the assumption that such an effort has value. In fact, members of the early scientific community clearly felt that gaining knowledge of their world was, in and of itself, a valuable activity. Early science was not simply an effort to achieve some material advantage or technological breakthrough. It was an adventure in the discovery of worldly happenings.[6]

A related characteristic of early modern science is that it was not merely an effort to gain knowledge about knowledge, as had been the case in certain Greek circles. Pioneers of modern science pursued knowledge about the physical universe in which they lived. They assumed that the world was a reality available for human inspection, understanding, and exploration. For them, it was immensely valuable simply to know more about it.

Two things about these assumptions are important. First, from the perspective of a pantheistic world view these assumptions can only be received with incredulity. What inherent value can there be in obtaining knowledge about something that is illusory and ultimately ephemeral? For the pantheist, the material world is an impediment to learning, not an object of value worthy of investigation. Indeed, it would not be an exaggeration to say that the pantheist gains true insight by finding release from worldly concern. Without in any way intending to be derogatory, therefore, we must conclude that there is neither incentive nor reason for science here.

Second, these assumptions are not only consistent with a Christian world view, they emanate directly from it. For the Christian, the world is valuable because God created it. He seared its value into the fabric of reality when He declared His creation to be good.[7] Thus, to acquire knowledge about the world is both to gain an understanding of worldly phenomena *and* an opportunity to catch a glimpse of God. Moreover, the God of creation established a certain kind of relationship between the world and humanity, a relationship that entailed specific responsibilities and opportunities for the human being. For example, the Creation account indicates that Adam and Eve were to take care of the Garden and name the animals, two tasks that assume much more than a passive knowledge of creation.[8] Indeed, I contend that the Christian who takes the Creation account seriously finds "worldly" learning to be not only meaningful but to some degree obligatory.

Beyond the assumption that the activity itself is valuable, however, there are other assumptions that appear necessary to the scientific enterprise. They can be divided into two groups. The first group consists of assumptions that have to do with the *type of world* being investigated, the second of assumptions concerning the *nature of the person* conducting the investigation.

One "type of world" assumption, for example, is the idea that the universe is orderly and uniform. Natural events do not occur haphazardly or unsystematically; regular patterns are normal and to be expected. The importance of this assumption is obvious but crucial. If there were no order or pattern to worldly events, there would be no way of explaining or predicting such phenomena.

This assumption of orderliness also implies that when a phenomenon is observed, one may assume that it resulted from the occurrence of a previous phenomenon. Thus, under normal conditions, the cause of one event is assumed to be another, preceding event. This assumption in a sense defines the field for the scientist and tells the scientist where to look for an explanation of any particular occurrence.

Assumptions must also be made about the "nature of the person" engaging in the scientific investigation. For one, it must be assumed that human beings can attain reliable knowledge through the senses. This means that the information gained by sense perception is generally reliable, especially if confirmed by a large number of consistent observations.[9] Without such an assumption, the scientist would be forced to cease all investigative activity; it is a basic methodological assumption.

Also important in this same category is the assumption that the human being's logical facilities can provide a reliable method of organizing knowledge. Thus, reasoning and inference become the tools by which the scientist categorizes, interprets, and theorizes. Without this assumption concerning human logic, one could neither impart meaning to one's research nor gain insight into possible directions for future research.

Though it is quite tempting to take these "type of world" and "nature of persons" assumptions for granted, we should not be misled into thinking that they are either obvious or universal. *They seem obvious to us only because they are common to our experience as twentieth-century people in the Western world.* The world is interpreted by us and for us through the perspective of these assumptions. They rarely are questioned, except at certain levels of philosophical speculation. Nevertheless, they are most definitely *faith assumptions,* beyond proof or indubitable understanding.

This point becomes more clear when we look at the presumed universality of these assumptions. On close inspection, it is obvious that people have not and do not always believe them. We need only to return to the pantheistic world view to see how they can be readily rejected. The pantheist, remember, assumes that the material world is ultimately illusory. This means that assumptions concerning the orderly nature of worldly phenomena are fundamentally irrelevant; they represent illegitimate speculation about nonexistent reality. Similarly, sense perceptions of worldly phenomena are at the very least irrelevant. Indeed, a devoted pantheist would argue that information gained through sense perception is fundamentally deceptive if it leads to an appreciation of the world as a distinct reality. For this reason also, human rationality is not something to be relied upon in the search for truth. Truth from a pantheistic perspective often presents itself as contradictory and ultimately illogical.

Finally, note once again how these assumptions derive implicitly from a Christian world view. One cannot fail to be impressed, for example, by the orderly nature of the universe as it is presented in the Genesis account. God creates a world in time intervals, with a variety of kinds, categories, and patterns. Not only that, but He creates a being in His image who is given the responsibility to continue the organizational process by naming the animals and tending the Garden. This creature is a sense-perceiving, feeling being, expected by the Creator to use its rational and sensual abilities to gain and employ knowledge about the creation.

Most important, God observes His creation and the being He has created and declares all of it to be good. In other words, God not only created the world and its human inhabitants, He also gave them attributes such as orderliness, and qualities such as sense perception and rationality, which are inherently valuable—characteristics that offer science a very healthy presuppositional undergirding.

CONCLUSION AND FOOTNOTE

I have argued in this chapter that modern science was nourished at the breast of a Christian world view. Its early development was nurtured primarily by Christian people whose faith was central to their interest in, and commitment to, science. Moreover, I have suggested that the assumptions that are prerequisite to modern science are Christian in character, implicitly and explicitly obtainable from a Christian world view.

I must admit at this point, however, that my analysis of the relationship between Christianity and early modern science has been somewhat one-sided—consciously so. It has emphasized the coherence and interrelatedness of this relationship and has ignored any real or perceived tension. But those familiar with the history of the church know that tensions between Christianity and science have often materialized. If modern science derived from a Christian world view, what explains the struggle that has often plagued this relationship? This is an important question, not only because it bears critically upon the thesis presented thus far, but also because its resolution helps explain the origins of the naturalistic approach to science.

Before we pursue this question, however, I want to once again specify the limits of the discussion. It seems to me that the tension between Christianity and science has been expressed on two levels, the first of which I shall call an "internal debate," the second, an "external debate." The *internal debate* is largely a dialogue among Christians concerning the nature of accepted truth. In essence, it involves a struggle between three legitimate sources of Christian truth—natural revelation (the world), special revelation (Scripture), and church history (the tradition of the church).

For the Christian, understanding truth has always involved the task of integrating the knowledge gained from those sources into an understandable, coherent package. Sometimes Christians have tried to gain coherence by simply jettisoning one source of truth if it seemed to contradict their own interpretation of reality. Scripture, church tradition, and worldly wisdom have all suffered such a fate at one time or another. More often, however, an integrative effort has been attempted and this, at times, has produced significant internal arguments. Much of the historical tension between Christianity and science, it seems, can be understood as a debate among Christians attempting to square their understanding of the world with their understanding of Scripture and church tradition. While this debate has always received a great deal of press (Galileo's predicament is one of the best known), it is not the one which is of most interest to us. For all its verbiage and ferocity, I see it as a perfectly normal and healthy dispute essential to the truth-gathering function of the church of Christ.

The next chapter, therefore, will ignore the dynamics of the internal debate in favor of the broader issues in the *external debate*. It is the latter that pits the Christian world view not against science but against the attempt to make modern science something quite different from the intentions of its earliest progenitors. This debate is the seed of the flower known as the naturalistic world view.

Chapter 4

THE IMPLICATIONS OF ASSUMPTIONS (II):

Christian Constraints and the Development of Science

The "external debate" has its origins in three Christian assumptions that at first glance may not appear to be particularly relevant to science. These assumptions concern three areas: the character of God, the manner in which He fashioned His human creation, and the present condition of this creation. I am convinced that they are the key to a fuller understanding of the relationship between Christianity and the development of science. For this discussion let us call them "Christian constraints" on science. Our task in this chapter will be twofold: to investigate the nature of Christian constraints on science and to understand how these constraints combined with historical events to bring about a naturalistic approach to science.

THE SCIENTIFIC CONTEXT: CHRISTIAN CONSTRAINTS

Up to this point, we have focused primarily on those assumptions within Christianity that served as a stimulant to and basis for modern science. There are other Christian assumptions, however, that serve as a limiting factor or control on the scientific enterprise. It should be pointed out that these are not in any sense in opposition to the earlier assumptions. Rather, they fulfill a different function. They present themselves in the form of constraints and guidelines to the development of science.

The first such assumption is that *God, as the Creator of the world, is greater than His creation.* For that reason, He is not bound or limited by its nature or characteristics *unless He chooses* to be so bound. The fact that He has created an orderly universe, for example, does not mean that He is confined by that order. Quite the reverse. It means that He might effect His will either by using the patterns He has established or, conversely, by contravening them altogether. "Miracle" is a popular term which we sometimes employ to describe such a contravention. While miracles do not appear to occur too often (if they did, they would cease to be miracles), the Christian tradition is replete with them. Thus, for the Christian, they are not only possible but clear historical occurrences.

For the scientist, the existence of miracles presents no particular problem or burden. It simply means that the assumption of an orderly universe cannot be taken as an absolute or ironclad given. Patterns and regularities are expected, but not altogether inevitable. Scientists working under this assumption, therefore, will shun absolutist claims in scientific research and remain cautiously open to other interpretations. They are not gullible, to be sure, but they are appropriately humble.

The second constraining assumption is actually a subpoint of the first. It emphasizes that *the human being, as one aspect of God's creation, is inferior to the Creator.* People were created as finite beings with limited capacities and abilities. To be sure, these abilities are substantial and significant; after all, God created humanity in His image. But man is not limitless. There are creational boundaries beyond which the human being cannot go.

This constraint is slightly more significant for science than the first. It means, for one thing, that limits exist which curb the knowledge-gathering capacity of the human being. Accordingly, there are some things the human being will never be able to understand or comprehend fully, simply because of his finitude.

These limits are not clearly defined, however, and they do not present themselves as clear-cut boundaries beyond which one cannot go. Rather, they entail the recognition that we are not God and that we will not, as finite beings, ever attain an understanding as complete or total as His. In a sense, while we are to pursue truth with all our strength, we are never to forget that God is the author of truth and that we are dependent upon Him for our understanding and knowledge. Once again, this beckons the scientist to a posture of humility regarding any truth claims made on the basis of scientific research. I might add parenthetically that it calls the theologian and all other human sojourners to precisely the same position.[1]

The assumption concerning human finitude has one other important implication. It confronts us with the possibility of error. Simply because we are human, we are prone to make unintended mistakes. For the scientific community, this means that there is always the possibility of a breakdown—in the collection of data, in the interpretation of events, in rational deliberation, and in theoretical prediction. Sense perception is not always reliable. Logic is not always foolproof. Things do go wrong (as Mr. Murphy is so keenly aware), and this assumption must also be integrated into a Christian view of science.

The final constraining assumption is probably the most significant. It presupposes *the existence and powerful influence of sin*. Up to this point, we have stressed over and over again that God created a good world. Now we must add an unfortunate ingredient. Through disobedience humanity fell from its intended position and became subject to the ravages of sin. This new condition does not alter the fact that human beings are created in the image of God and as such are still of great worth and possess the potential for good works. But it does open up the possibility, indeed the inevitability, of human life being governed by self-centered rather than God-centered motives. The world has become vulnerable to the effects of evil.

The consequences of this assumption are nothing short of profound. First, it means that error is not only the possible result of human finitude, but it may emanate directly from intentional deception. People lie. That, in its bluntest form, is the crux of the problem. This tendency is every bit as potent among scientists as other human beings. Deception, moreover, is not simply bald-faced fabrication. It may take the form of a subtle maneuver to convince the scientific community of a "fact" or "hypothesis" out of purely selfish motives, without concern for or appreciation of truth. A scientist operating under the assumption of sin must always recognize the possibility of intentional error within the scientific literature.

The effect of sin, however, is not limited to error. It is also evident in certain clever uses of truth. We see this, for example, in the appeal to scientific knowledge to support a false conclusion (e.g., "American Indians have lower average S.A.T. scores than white Americans, therefore they are genetically inferior"). It surfaces as well in situations where information is employed for essentially evil purposes (e.g., "Since Indians are inferior, we should exclude them from the privileges of American society").

Finally, knowledge about the world may be used to glorify the creation rather than the Creator. Most often this occurs through attempts to honor the observer (i.e., the scientist) rather than the one who designed that which is being observed, but it can also be accomplished through an understanding of creation as an autonomous phenomenon void of its Creator. In any case, the Christian world view confronts us with this revelation: knowledge is not naive. Rather, it comes to us in loaded form, full of motivation, intention, and implication.

A NATURALISTIC APPROACH TO SCIENCE

Up to this point we have argued that science grew out of a Christian world view, in part because the assumptions of this world view provided very fertile soil for scientific thinking. But this world view also placed science in a particular kind of context, one in which science is perceived not as some type of god but as an attempt to understand and appreciate God's creation. It is a perspective that includes the possibility of divine contraventions of the natural order, the probability of intentional and unintentional error, and the inevitability of loaded (value-laden) knowledge. In short, Christian science includes Christian constraints.

As the scientific effort developed and expanded, however, a segment of the scientific community came to see some or all of these Christian constraints as shackles to the full flowering of science. In general, these individuals were a product of the Enlightenment, and they carried Enlightenment thinking into the heart of science.[2] While we do not have the time to detail either the form or content of Enlightenment thought, it is important to know that its pivotal assumption concerned the centrality of the human being. It placed ultimate meaning and responsibility on the shoulders of humanity.[3] Human beings were viewed as the creators of their own future, the source of their own fulfillment.

As a consequence, any perspective that tended to shift the focus away from humanity (to God, for example) was suspect and counterproductive to the goals of the Enlightenment. Thus, religion was not only seen as wrong thinking but as the source of many of humanity's difficulties. It inhibited the believer from recognizing his obligation to shape his own destiny.

Two assumptions within the Christian world view were particularly anathema to Enlightenment thinking. The first was the idea that created beings (humanity) were dependent upon the Creator (God); the second was the notion of sin and human depravity. From the Enlightenment perspective, the first assumption threatened human autonomy and the second undermined the concept of human progress. More important, both notions removed the human being from center stage and struck at the heart of the Enlightenment concept of humanity. They had to go.

And go they did. Not only in philosophical speculation but, eventually, in science as well. In effect, when Enlightenment thinking penetrated the scientific community, it thereby excluded Christian constraints from the scientific enterprise. As a result, it transformed science from a means of understanding God's creation into a source of human exaltation, freedom, and progress. From the Enlightenment perspective, science without constraints was a potentially omnipotent force, one that could solve all mystery and bring about the salvation of the human race. Free of its Christian roots and in the arms of the Enlightenment, science had the possibility of realizing its full potential.

But we are jumping ahead of the story, for the immediate impact of this development on science was not a headlong rush to embrace Enlightenment thinking. Too many scientists were philosophically predisposed in other directions to make such a move possible. Rather, the first effect of the Enlightenment was the separation of Christianity from science and the acceptance of the related idea that religion and science should not be entangled. This was an extremely important step. It was accomplished and justified by another notion, namely, that science can and must be value free—a position sometimes termed "objective science."[4]

Because of widespread confusion over the concept of objective science we need to be clear about its meaning and implications. The advocates of objective science, of course, believe objectivity is essential for the existence of an unbiased science. For that reason, the concept of objective science is sometimes assumed to be the cornerstone of scientific honesty and truth, the only sure defense against prejudiced research. However, it should be apparent by now that I believe all knowledge is prejudiced in the sense that it is value-laden and permeated by a priori assumptions.

This is not to say that scientists must or should be unconcerned about issues of honesty and truthfulness in scientific research. They certainly should be. But scientific honesty is a distinct and separate issue from objective science. The first is a personal predisposition influenced by the scientist's commitment to an ethical or moral system—not to objective science. The latter is a philosophical position that rests on the assumption that one can engage in science without regard to larger world view presuppositions. It views science as an autonomous activity quite separate from any consideration of world view.

Consequently, with the acceptance of objective science within the scientific community, two important things happened. First, a new norm was adopted, one that required the scientist to abandon religious preconceptions when donning his or her scientific smock. Second, science was effectively cut off from its Christian roots and grafted onto a new root structure, a foundation that I will call the naturalistic world view.

This second event requires some elaboration. Why did the acceptance of objective science mean the adoption of a naturalistic approach to science? What accounts for this transformation? When Christianity was cut off from science, two crucial things occurred. First, the operational assumptions of science were elevated from general guidelines to absolute presuppositions. Second, without Christianity as its context, science no longer operated within the orbit of Christian constraints. Both of these developments are significant and worthy of our understanding.

Once science was divorced from religious ideas, the nature and meaning of science remained in question. This is because Christianity had provided science with not only its nourishment but also its *raison d'être*. Without this undergirding, science was in need of an "objective" (nonreligious) philosophical context. That context was provided by the operational assumptions to which it was already wedded.

By operational assumptions we simply mean those postulates which, from a Christian perspective, provide guidance and direction to the operation of scientific discovery (e.g., nature is orderly and uniform; natural events have natural causes; adequate knowledge can be derived through the use of human sense perception). Within the context of a Christian world view these assumptions were not the source of ultimate faith. They were, rather, general tendencies in the world based upon the character of God and the nature of His creation. Separated from that context, however, they were no longer general tendencies; they became absolute truth. Thus, these operational assumptions were transformed into incontrovertible, presuppositional realities.

For example, consider the assumption concerning the orderly nature of the world. Within this new scientific perspective, the reason nature can be assumed to be orderly no longer was that it was created as a part of an orderly universe. That would be a religious assumption. Rather, nature is assumed to be orderly because that is the way it presents itself to the perceiver. In other words, it is orderly because that is its fundamental nature. Suddenly we move from a creational tendency to an absolute statement that defines the very essence of reality. Note that its reason for being true is a purely materialistic one. It is a "fact" because *that is the way things are.* No other reasons are necessary, nor can they be entertained in the context of this new scientific perspective.

The second consequence of the separation of science and Christianity was the elimination of Christian constraints. In effect, this converted the scientific enterprise from a *means of understanding* to an *end*—that is, an object worthy of our adoration and capable of extricating humanity from its basic predicament. This change had three noteworthy effects.

First, the elimination of Christian constraints meant that the scientist as a scientist was no longer permitted to consider the possibility of divine intervention (miracles) in a natural process. God was expressly forbidden to enter the domain of scientific explanation. Not only did this mean that miracles were now considered a scientific impossibility, it also implied on a more subtle level that natural events operate mechanistically and outside the sovereignty of God.

Second, the exclusion of Christian constraints also eliminated the concept of the scientist as necessarily limited in his or her ability to acquire knowledge. This does not mean that all scientists working under the new science consider themselves gods (though some appear to at times). It does mean, however, that previously assumed creational limits to knowledge acquisition no long exist. Thus the door is open to ultimate truth claims in scientific study—claims that were not possible within the context of Christian constraints. This in effect diminishes scientific humility and discourages cautious application of scientific discoveries.

Finally, the abandoning of Christian constraints meant that the concept of sin was no longer considered in scientific discourse. This inspired still further confidence in scientific revelation, and it also allowed scientific knowledge to be viewed as uncontaminated knowledge—as pure fact. Science was now conceived as existing outside the domain of morality, completely unbiased and neutral. In short, science was now objective truth.

CONCLUSION

What we have then in objective science is nothing less than a new world view, with its own postulates of faith, yet without a religious label. It is quite clearly a naturalistic world view. It assumes that the material world is the sum total of reality; no other reality is worthy of consideration.

Two additional points need to be stressed. First, the changes that occurred with the development of objective science were not insignificant. They brought about a radical shift in the nature and meaning of science. This point needs to be emphasized because, at one level of analysis, the changes may appear minor. After all, the presuppositions of objective science are similar to the derived assumptions of a Christian approach to science.

What must be kept in mind, however, is that with the shift came a completely new interpretive framework, one that eliminated transcendent reality as well as Christian constraints. To grasp the significance of that change, one only needs to review the primary assumptions of a naturalistic world view (chap. 2). These are the postulates of faith on which the new science operates, and they are radically different from a Christian world view. If, as we have repeatedly argued, assumptions affect conclusions, then objective science will have results markedly different from a Christian approach to science.

Second, precisely because objective science presents itself as neutral or unbiased, it is highly dogmatic and, indeed, authoritarian. It requires scientists to work within its assumptive framework and denies the legitimacy of other approaches to science. The modern scientist is told to operate on the basis of objective science, ostensibly to assure unbiased results (i.e., results that conform to a naturalistic world view). It "generously" allows scientists to hold contrary world views in their personal lives but ardently denies them that right in the realm of science. Only one individual is given the freedom and privilege of complete integrity, where personal and professional assumptions coincide. That person, of course, is the naturalist. All others are condemned to live a life of philosophical schizophrenia—or to convert.

Chapter 5

ON THE STATE OF OBJECTIVE SCIENCE: TROUBLE IN PARADISE

But what if objective science is possible after all? Regardless of the historical circumstances surrounding the development of objective science, what if it is possible to study the world in a value-free manner, without regard to questions of ultimate reality?

That is a crucial question, one not yet fully addressed in this book. For if a neutral science is attainable, then the claim that objective science is a front for naturalism is a lie, and the argument for a Christian approach to science is wrong. Indeed, if a philosophically detached position is feasible, then it ought to be a prerequisite to good science, and those who do otherwise ought to be exposed as dangerous folks: they undermine the activities of truth-loving scientists everywhere. If objective science is possible, then its adherents have a right to be dogmatic.

To no one's surprise, I am more than a little dubious about the potential of objective science. This skepticism, however, is not shared by the whole of the Western world. In fact, at various times during the last few centuries, the specter of an omnipotent science has loomed large in the Western mind. Freed from direct Christian influence, buoyed by Enlightenment optimism, and confident in its rational faith, objective

science has at one time or another been deemed savior of
mankind, master of mystery, and the hope of future generations. Central to this hyperbole is the idea that naturalistic
science has an unlimited capacity to explain the world and to
reveal truth. It is an idea that has generated a great deal of
euphoria—and not a few difficulties. In this chapter, we will
look at three such difficulties: the problem of certainty, the
problem of relativity, and the problem of consequentiality.

THE PROBLEM OF CERTAINTY

From the beginning there have been those who have raised
what I call the problem of certainty. In general terms, this is the
question of how human beings know something to be true. Of
course, this problem did not originate with objective science. It
represents an age-old debate and is a question to which many
answers have been given. But the issue is particularly crucial
within objective science because of the manner in which the
latter attempts to legitimize its position within the scientific
academy.

Remember that objective science differentiates itself from
other ways of knowing by virtue of its unbiased or value-free
character. Its proponents argue that it is an approach to
knowing that does not presuppose any articles of faith that
cannot be empirically demonstrated. In other words, it claims
that it only requires its adherents to assume those things that
can be known *with certainty*. All other knowledge, it asserts, is
not a part of objective science. In this way it divides the world
of knowledge into two categories—that which we understand
by speculation (intuition, feelings, religion, myth, etc.) and that
which we know with certainty (science).

In its most elementary form, the central problem with this
assertion of objective science is that it simply is not demonstrable. Ever since the early criticisms of David Hume,[1] the
advocates of objective science have been unable to show that
their assumptions are either indubitably true or in any sense
"faith-less." While a discussion of the exact nature of this
problem is beyond our scope here, a brief example may be
helpful.

As stated before, the scientist assumes that nature is orderly and that natural events have natural causes. We noted, as well, that these are foundational assumptions in objective science. They seem to be obviously true—the kind of thing that we can know with certainty. But, indeed, can we? For example, even if we think that we know with certainty that Natural Event A caused Natural Event B (ostensibly because of observed repetitive occurrences), does that demonstrate that natural events have natural causes? No, it does not, because we do not know whether there exists somewhere in the universe a contradictory phenomenon. We could repeat similar types of experiments a million times, get the same results each time, and we would still not know for certain that the general proposition was true.

But the problem really goes much deeper than this. Continuing with the above example, we cannot even know with certainty that Natural Event A caused Natural Event B. Though we may have observed a relationship between A and B, for example, we do not know if under different circumstances the relationship would exist or whether we are really perceiving (with our eyes, possibly) what we think we are perceiving. This has led some (Karl Popper in particular)[2] to argue that, while we cannot know that a causal relationship exists, we can know at times that a causal relationship does not exist. But even this approach, sometimes called "falsificationism," is problematic. It not only fails to deal with the perceptual problem, but also, as Wolterstorff points out, it "seldom instructs us to reject a theory. For seldom are theories shown to be inconsistent with what is taken as foundation."[3] In other words, there seem to be limitless ways for the human being (scientist, in this case) to explain why A may still cause B even though we observed a phenomenon which, in one situation, appeared to contradict such a thing. In short, we cannot even reject a scientific theory with certainty, much less affirm one.

What must be concluded from all of this, it would appear, is that the postulates of objective science cannot be approached as certain truth. Rather, they are faith assumptions, accepted as truth for whatever reason but not known indubitably as truth. It should be noted, of course, that our argument does not demonstrate, or even suggest, that these postulates are false. They may, indeed, be true, but they cannot be shown to be so with certainty. What I have tried to show, however, is that the distinction between objective scientific knowledge and all other knowledge, based on the claim that the latter is based on faith and the former is not, seems to be erroneous. All knowledge requires faith (including the sentence you are trying to comprehend at this moment).

THE PROBLEM OF RELATIVITY

Despite the fact that the problem of certainty has been raised in one form or another ever since the seventeenth century, most advocates of objective science have chosen to either ignore or circumvent the problem. Though the second alternative has consistently failed, the first has been immensely successful. In part, ignorance of the problem of certainty was made easy by the spectacular technological achievements associated with nineteenth- and twentieth-century science. Thus, as we moved into the middle of the twentieth century, the meaning, dignity, and status of science seemed fairly secure. Indeed, for some it was nothing short of an exercise in majesty to even be a part of this quest for knowledge. The basis for this pride was a conception of science often believed by the laymen and fostered by the advocates of objective science.

Typical of this conception of science might be the following definitive statement: Science is the systematic and empirical discovery of verifiable general laws in the natural world. As such, science is a cumulative discipline where each empirical discovery builds upon those findings which preceded it. Science is both evolutionary and pyramidal—evolutionary in that it is increasingly capable of explaining our world in ever more succinct language, and pyramidal because this evolution allows for the rapid, vertical building of knowledge on a continually broadening base.

Majestic though this conception may be, it was dealt a heavy blow in 1962 with the publication of Thomas Kuhn's *The Structure of Scientific Revolutions*.[4] Kuhn's thesis is that science does not develop cumulatively, but changes as a result of revolutions—scientific revolutions. At any given point in time, says Kuhn, science is dominated by a particular paradigm (the basic image of a science's subject matter—the glasses through which the scientist looks at his subject). For a period of time, the accuracy of the paradigm is assumed by the scientific community. However, as new research findings are generated by the community, some do not fit well within the existing paradigm (they are "unexplainable"). A crisis occurs when so many of these unexplainable findings arise that people begin looking for explanations outside of the existing paradigm. A radical change (a "scientific revolution") takes place, therefore, when the scientific community shifts its allegiance from the reigning paradigm to a new paradigm that demonstrates itself capable of explaining the existing anomalies.

An example may be helpful. Newtonian physics was the dominant paradigm in physics from about 1600 to 1900. As time passed, however, it became clear that the Newtonian framework was incapable of explaining a growing number of findings in physics. With Einstein came a new paradigm that seemed to explain not only Newtonian physics but some of the "unexplainables" as well. A scientific revolution occurred, according to Kuhn, when the scientific community scrambled to embrace its new paradigm.

What is the significance of Kuhn's analysis? First of all, if Kuhn's thesis is correct, scientific progress is much more relative than the advocates of objective science had ever imagined it to be. Scientific truth in Kuhn's hands is "truth in relation to a particular paradigm"; it is not "scientific truth—period." The insights of science are not necessarily wrong, but they are *perspectives on truth* rather than absolute truths in and of themselves.

Second, it demonstrates that scientific "progress" (or, more accurately, "change") is more sociological than inexorable. In other words, changes within science follow certain general patterns associated with social change, rather than some unique pattern of scientific change. Ideological shifts within the scientific community, for example, proceed very much like political changes within every community; the "progress" of science is not sociologically unique.

Finally, Kuhn's analysis shows, once again, the important role assumptions play in the ongoing development of science. As Masterman makes clear, when Kuhn asserts that paradigms are ways of seeing the subject matter, he is arguing that paradigms are metaphysical categories delimiting scientific behavior on the basis of a priori assumptions.[5] More simply put, the paradigms define what is of concern to scientists, where to look (and where *not* to look) for answers, and what scientists can expect to find at the end of their search. In short, the findings of objective science are highly influenced by paradigmatic assumptions.

Once again, please note that the problem of relativity, like the problem of certainty, tells us very little about the truthfulness of objective science. Though we are sometimes prone to doubt the credibility of relative truth, we have no business doing so on that basis alone.[6]

What we have discovered, however, is that objective science is not the entity it generally is thought to be. First, its assumptions are not certain; they are matters of faith, as are all such assumptions. Second, the findings of science cannot be described as objective truth. They are instead relative insights, dependent upon both metaphysical and theoretical assumptions, which also require faith. Both of these points indicate that there is really nothing neutral or objective about objective science. It is, instead, a transparently naturalistic approach to science, one which assumes naturalistic presuppositions and leads to naturalistic conclusions.

THE PROBLEM OF CONSEQUENTIALITY

The philosophical questions raised by the problems of certainty and relativity are not unique to objective science; they are problematic for all approaches to knowledge and truth. Indeed, they are a significant part of our discussion only because many of the advocates of objective science have tried to deny their applicability to that enterprise. Once these denials have been laid to rest, however, we are still left with the question of consequentiality: What have been the results of objective (naturalistic) science? This is not so much a philosophical issue as a pragmatic one. To use a metaphor, we are interested in evaluating the tree by the fruit it produces.

To illustrate the problem of consequentiality, I want to discuss an issue that resulted from the writings of Charles Darwin. There is a certain risk in using this example since even after nearly a century and a half Darwin's ideas still produce great amounts of emotional rhetoric. My concern here, however, is not the question of evolution per se, but rather to learn of the consequences of naturalistic thinking in science. For that purpose alone the case of Darwin is most insightful.

At the outset, I should say that from a Christian perspective the significance of Darwin is not his understanding of the process of natural selection. Whether or not God chose, and is choosing, to create the world in that fashion, though terribly interesting, is not a crucial metaphysical issue for the Christian scientist. The Christian world view does not dictate one's position on the question of natural selection, nor does the acceptance or rejection of Darwinian theory affect the Christian scientist's understanding of origins. In either case, God remains the Creator.

The naturalist, however, does not have this same luxury of choice. Once accepted, the theory of evolution almost inevitably becomes not only a description of the development of life forms but also an explanation of beginnings. In other words, it becomes by default a crucial metaphysical assumption. This is because the naturalistic perspective assumes a strictly materialistic explanatory context. The naturalist, therefore, must have an explanation of origins that assumes only the existence of prior materialistic conditions. When spied from a naturalistic world view, natural selection fits the bill precisely. Thus, the logic of naturalism nearly compels all those employing its assumptions, *including objective scientists*, to view Darwinian theory as an answer to the questions of origin.

Surely one of the great ironies of history is that the people who had the luxury of choice on this issue (Christians) were the ones who were labeled "dogmatists," while the ones who were saddled with no options at all (naturalists) were those who coveted the title of "liberals." No doubt it is an irony brought about in large measure by those Christians who interpreted the

findings of Darwin as heretical and contrary to the teachings of
Scripture. But I would stress that this particular "Christian"
interpretation of Darwin was only partly due to a certain
theological bent (the twenty-four-hour-day interpretation of
Genesis). What is just as important in the Christian reaction is
the tendency of many Christians within the scientific community to interpret the data *from the perspective of objective science*
(naturalism). Thus, when these Christians donned the cloak of
objective science, they readily perceived the implications of
evolutionary thinking even if they did not see the naturalistic
assumptions that were leading them to such conclusions. We
should not be surprised, therefore, to find that these same
Christians felt compelled either to reject the Darwinian interpretation of the data (and thus the theory of evolution) or to
reject their Christian faith.

If there is one remaining irony in all of this, however, it
must be that the hubbub surrounding the "Christian" reaction
to evolution has often blinded us to the far-reaching implications of such thinking for objective science. For while the issue
is a nuisance to some Christian apologists, it illuminates and
exemplifies a number of deep crises ("problems of consequentiality") within the naturalistic community of objective science.

Crisis of meaning. Though the advocates of naturalism
hailed the discoveries of Darwin as evidence supporting their
world view, some objective scientists were quick to pick up
troubling implications. For one thing, if the origins of life could
be explained in terms of objective science, then the world was
indeed an exclusively material reality. This conclusion, of
course, was essentially tautological, since it resulted from
naturalistic presuppositions in the first place. However, for
objective scientists who thought they were operating on the
basis of neutral assumptions, this was a devastating discovery.
For now they felt that objective science had proven the reality
of naturalistic assumptions.

This discovery meant that many objective scientists were
for the first time confronted by a crisis of meaning. They
realized, for example, that they now had to confine their
meaning context to the material world—not only as scientists
but as human beings. They could no longer transcend the

natural context in their search for meaning. God could not give them that meaning and, as was learned sometime later, neither could the nation (in the naturalist sense) or man (in the humanist sense). Truth could only be understood in terms of what they perceived as natural. And if this news was not depressing enough, the more perceptive were to realize that even their newly discovered foundation of naturalistic presuppositions was subject to the problems of certainty and relativity. For a few, all of this bad news merely meant that humanity had finally come of age. For those who wanted more from life, however, it meant that, indeed, there was trouble in paradise.

Crisis of Direction. But trouble was not limited to the crisis of meaning; that was only the beginning. The debate over evolution made it quite clear that human beings could not escape the implications of naturalistic thinking, either as interpreters of its meaning or as subjects. The crisis of meaning had also become a "crisis of direction," for it was apparent that objective science could not safely confine its analysis to nonhuman phenomena. Its theories had to apply to human beings precisely as they did to everything else, since naturalistic assumptions provided no basis whatsoever to understand them differently. This realization opened the floodgates to a wholesale naturalistic understanding of humanity, not only in the physical sciences but also in history, politics, economics, psychology, anthropology, and sociology. The conquest of humanity had begun. It was a disturbing thought to those objective scientists who desperately wanted there to be something unique about the human being. But naturalism had come home to roost and its direction could not be altered.

Crisis in Ethics. The crises of meaning and direction implied at least one remaining problem—what I call a "crisis in ethics." To put it boldly (despite protests to the contrary), there are simply no inherent ethical parameters in naturalistic (objective) science. The key word here is "inherent." While naturalists may bring external ethical considerations to science, they will find none within their own world view. If reality is totally material, and if humanity is an unexceptional part of that natural world, then ethical or other values are nothing more than an expression of the human organism's material interests. They do not constitute an ethic.

At this point, some might argue that moral systems can be explained naturalistically in terms of humanity's desire for self-preservation. Thus, survival depends upon stable relationships and the latter depend upon an established moral order. But this seems at best nothing more than a naturalistic description of the origin and functioning of morality. It does not tell John Q. Scientist why he should practice a particular ethic, except as it is in his own self-interest. If he decides, however, that it is in his self-interest to practice deception or anything else, then there is nothing to contain his behavior and no higher morality to which he can appeal. Such an approach, it appears, fails to provide the kind of guidance that we normally expect and assume from a legitimate ethical system.

This crisis in ethics was painfully evident during the reign of the Third Reich in Germany. Some of the best, most talented objective scientists in Europe were willing to experiment on fellow human beings regardless of the consequences because it would further science and the nation. From a naturalistic perspective, there is simply no way one can condemn their actions. They were expanding the horizons of science; they were certainly acting on the basis of self-preservation. But they were murdering other human beings. Though most contemporary naturalists would condemn such behavior, their world view gives them no basis for doing so.[7] And this, when all is said and done, may be the most troubling consequence of a naturalistic approach to science.

CONCLUSION

Is objective science feasible? If by "objective" one means a philosophically neutral or assumption-free science, then I think that the answer is no. The problem of certainty suggests that there is nothing we can know with certitude, including the insights of science. We approach all knowledge with a modicum of faith—faith in perception, logic, the reality of the thing we study, and so forth. Thus, the claim that objective science is value-free appears to be bogus.

Similarly, the assumed neutrality of objective science seems erroneous. The problem of relativity indicates that the findings of science are themselves conditioned by the paradigms through which they are viewed. The sun which appears to be traveling around the earth within one set of assumptions seems to be doing nothing of the sort within another. There is no direct connection between what we see and truth; the line is full of switchboards and operators, each making a significant contribution to our understanding of both the seeing and the truth. The claim, then, that objective science somehow removes the need for "switchboards and operators"—or has at its disposal the only neutral or truthful switchboard operators—would also seem to be a bogus claim.

When these insights are coupled with those of the previous chapter, it is difficult to escape the conclusion that objective science is neither neutral nor value-free but quite explicitly naturalistic. Failure to recognize the naturalistic character of objective science, however, has led to a number of significant problems. Among Christians, it has often resulted in the belief that science is an enemy of faith—a discipline continually undermining Christian interpretations of reality. Some of these problems are no doubt an offshoot of theological disputes within the church (the *internal debate*). Yet, in large measure, the undermining aspect of science is the result of the patently naturalistic assumptions being employed by the so-called objective scientist. The enemy of faith is not science; rather, the problem is a naturalistic study of God's creation.

The cloak of objective science has been problematic for more than just the Christian, however. As we have seen, for the objective scientist who desires more of a world view than materialistic reductionism, the naturalistic explanations of objective science have led to a crisis of meaning. Similarly, for those who assumed or hoped for the uniqueness of humanity, the increasing ability of objective science to provide naturalistic explanations for human activity has spawned a crisis of direction. And finally, for those who understand the importance of ethics in science, the ability of objective science to explain this need in naturalistic categories has created a crisis of ethics. In short, some objective scientists, who expected more of their disciplines than naturalistic implications, have been disappointed by the work of their own hands.

Chapter 6

ON THE STATE OF THE SOCIAL SCIENCES: ONE CHRISTIAN'S ASSESSMENT

The reader may still wonder about the actual consequences of the problems of objective science outlined in the preceding chapter. After all, the problems of certainty and relativity are not unique to objective science, and not a few Christians have been known to engage in questionable ethical activities. Suppose objective science *is* inherently naturalistic. Suppose its assumptions are not quite what they pretend to be—that they are a little less than certain and more than a little "faith-full." Is that really so problematic? After all, what do such problems have to do with the stuff of science—the everyday findings and discoveries of the contemporary scholar? Specifically, of what importance are they to the human or social sciences—those disciplines claiming to take the study of the human condition seriously?[1]

Given what has been said so far, my opinions should be clear: if objective science is inherently naturalistic, then it is also less than Christian; if its assumptions are not what they purport to be, then they are more than a little fraudulent; and, if assumptions about ultimate reality affect the way we think and behave, then the stuff of science will be significantly shaped by the naturalistic assumptions of objective science, whether in the physical or human sciences.

Still, for many these remain important questions. In this chapter, therefore, we will try to put some flesh on the skeleton already assembled and come to grips with the consequences of objective science for the human or social sciences. In order to accomplish this, we will first look briefly at the context within which the social sciences took shape; second, investigate the effect of this context on the assumptions of the modern social scientist; and finally consider the consequences of these assumptions for social science method, theory, and application. Before proceeding, however, let me include a word of caution. No single chapter can adequately treat a topic of this magnitude and no pretense of accomplishing that task is made here. Rather, our purpose is primarily to explain and to illustrate— providing an accurate rendering of the "forest," we trust, but making no claim concerning the "trees."[2]

CONCEIVED IN LIBERTY

In order to understand the state of the social sciences today, it is important to keep the following point in mind: The scientific study of the human condition began in earnest *after* the shift to objective science was already complete. Certainly aspects of humanity were studied before the advent of Western science. In fact, there exists a veritable feast of social and political thought which is both profoundly premodern and quite insightful.[3] Nevertheless, the "sciences of man" are fundamentally nineteenth- and twentieth-century phenomena. This is not to say that earlier concepts were unimportant to the development of the social sciences. Quite clearly many of the initial attempts at social science were rooted in philosophical disputes of the seventeenth and eighteenth centuries. What I am asserting, however, is that the human sciences gained their legitimacy and contemporary form during a period of time when objective science was preeminent.

This assertion is most readily evident in the histories of psychology and sociology, since both disciplines took shape in the nineteenth and twentieth centuries. Once again, this does not mean that pre-nineteenth-century thinking was irrelevant to the evolution of psychology or sociology. It does mean, however, that these two disciplines are decisively modern endeavors, constituted within the context of objective science.

One might contend, of course, that our argument is less persuasive in economics, since there is at least a perceptible link between Greek, medieval, early modern, and modern economics. One also might argue that it is least true in political science, where there is a long tradition of political philosophy. Nevertheless, even in these more established disciplines the present conception of the task (e.g., purpose and method) is almost always defined in the modern terms of objective science. This is especially the case in economics, where one sometimes gets the feeling that premodern economic thought is of more value today for its "straw man" potential than for its view of the economy. Pick up an introductory text on economics—or on any of the other social sciences, for that matter—and count the number of pages devoted to premodern insights. Then count the number of those insights considered valuable in modern science. The point is this: Regardless of their somewhat diverse historical circumstances, the social sciences defined themselves as "sciences" during a time when objective science was their raison d'être. Thus they sought their legitimacy in the context of a naturalistic world view.

The crucial question, of course, is, What are the implications of all this? If our argument is correct, then we must conclude that the human sciences were conceived in liberty from the overt influence of a Christian world view. Being confident that this conclusion will be misunderstood, let me qualify it briefly before proceeding to a discussion of its consequences.

First, my assertion that the social sciences were established outside the direct influence of a Christian world view is quite different from saying that the social sciences were conceived either in opposition to Christianity or free of Christian influence. Indeed, if our argument is correct, then one could say that the human sciences took shape within the context of a mutant form of Christian assumptions. Remember, the assumptions of objective science were, by and large, derived from a Christian world view. They were the operational assumptions of a Christian understanding of the world yet devoid of

Christian constraints. So the point is not that objective science is antichristian in every detail or that its assumptions are totally without merit. I am simply saying that taken as a whole—as an interpretive framework—objective science is not a Christian perspective on science.

Second, my thesis that the social sciences took shape outside of a Christian world view does not imply that Christians were absent or uninvolved in its origins. In fact, one can discover a small number of what we must assume are honest Christians in the formative stages of most of the human sciences.[4] Our argument is not that the human sciences were conceived without the help of Christians but that they came into being without the overt influence of a Christian world view. The two are quite different. There are Christians everywhere who approach their businesses or professions as utilitarians, hedonists, or whatever; similarly, the Christian scientist is quite capable of being a Christian without applying the implications of Christian thought to his or her discipline. Certainly my own biography suggests that I am capable of such a thing.[5] Likewise, the history of the early development of the human sciences would indicate that many Christian social scientists were and still are able to divorce many of the implications of their world view from the world of science.

Lest we be too harsh, it would be well to remember that in following this course of action these Christian social scientists were merely marching to the beat of the broader scientific community; that is, they were being consistent with their social base. To expect more of them is to expect more than the majority of Christians have been able to carry off for most of the history of Christianity. Moreover, most Christian objective scientists believed and still believe that by being objective they were protecting social science from prejudice and bias—an obviously good goal. It is easy to see, therefore, how they might have been seduced into the arms of objective social science. Nevertheless, understandable or not, this means that in its formative years the study of humanity was being nurtured and carried out by a group of brilliant scholars who were functionally ignorant of the fact that the object of their study was created *imago Dei*, in God's image.

THE IRRELEVANT GOD

The consequences of this fact were not insignificant. It means, for one thing, that the social sciences were established in the "theoretical" absence of God. As pivotal questions were being formulated about method (How shall we study humanity?), data (What is the nature of the "thing" we study?), and meaning (How shall we interpret the results of our research and where shall we look for further insights?), the God of the universe was assumed to be irrelevant, uninterested, or nonexistent. To employ a biblical metaphor, as the pot was about to study itself, it assumed that the existence or wisdom of the Potter was irrelevant to the task. It was an assumption for which the pot would pay dearly.

First, it meant that the study of humanity was locked into a methodology that assumed a closed system of cause and effect. That is, it presupposed that any human pattern of behavior or thought could be explained purely in terms of prior, material, perceptible conditions. The form of this determinism varied from discipline to discipline (environment, social class, instinct, etc.), but the consequences were the same. The study of humanity became fused with the assumption that the human being could be explained via naturalistic categories. This assumption prevailed, by the way, in spite of the fact that few such naturalistic theories were actually able to "explain the variance" (i.e., account for the phenomenon under investigation) and few social scientists genuinely hoped they would. Nevertheless, despite the lack of explanatory success (economists and experimental psychologists to the contrary notwithstanding), and despite the fact that many social and behavioral scientists seemed to harbor deep-seated fears about the implications of complete success, the march of this closed methodological system continues to this day, unimpeded by fear or failure. Its popularity, even in the face of contradictory evidence, is testimony to the power of the naturalistic world view in the modern social sciences.

Second, the irrelevance of God implied that the data (humanity) could be studied apart from any notion of transcendent connections. Thus, the human sciences assumed that the human being was an autonomous "thing," unaffected by the influences of a Creator. Such an assumption is not only incorrect from a Christian perspective, but it has also reaped a whirlwind of reductionist methodology. This view of humanity, for example, has enabled social scientists to take a concept such as "love" and, in the process of gathering data on the subject, reduce it to a conditioned response, a false consciousness, a biological need, a specific behavioral pattern, or an answer on a survey questionnaire. If one disregards the biblical picture of humanity—or, for that matter, if one is willing to set aside altogether the wisdom of the Ancients— then any method that makes love observable or quantifiable is perfectly justified. The fact that it badly disfigures the human image is irrelevant or, worse yet, disputed.

For the Christian, of course, the problem here is *not* the interest of the modern scientist in the physiological, psychological, or social influences upon concepts or expressions of love. Rather, it is the modern assumption that one can gain an adequate understanding of love by employing such methods. It is not, for example, the survey method I find offensive, but the assumption that the results are anything more than the collective attitudes of a segment of the population on the subject of love.

Third, the irrelevance of God in the human sciences also implied that theoretical meaning could be ascribed only in natural categories. Thus, if I am a social scientist engaged in the study of religion (or economics, or government), I am required to interpret the phenomenon as if it occurred in a transcendent void. An objective sociologist studying Christian conversions in Korea, for example, is not only limited to an investigation of the social exigencies of Christian conversion (a perfectly proper limitation as long as the sociologist recognizes that he or she is studying only one segment of the phenomenon), but also is compelled to develop interpretations on the assumption that the activity of God is wholly irrelevant to the event in question.

The more sensitive sociologist, of course, may preface such an interpretation with the disclaimer that an objective scientist cannot pass judgment on the validity of a religious belief and must base interpretation upon empirical evidence only.[6] While such a disclaimer may satisfy the intellect of the naive (which, in this case, includes the social scientist), it does no such thing for the religious convert (the subject of the study). The Christian who has had a "Damascus Road experience" knows that the objective interpretation of his experience (1) logically contradicts his own interpretation and, therefore, in fact passes judgment on its validity; and (2) assumes that the convert's interpretation of his experience is not based on empirical evidence. From the convert's perspective, the objective interpretation is not only not neutral, it is incorrect.[7] Indeed, only the objective scientist's audience will assume the sociologist's insights to be neutral—all the while shaking their heads in dismay at the way Koreans are imbibing the myths of the Christian faith.

The use of a religious example should not deter us from the broader implications. Not only the objective interpretations of religious events are inappropriately naturalistic—objective interpretations of *all* human events are inappropriately naturalistic. The Christian scholar should be every bit as uncomfortable with a godless interpretation of government or economics as of Christian conversion. Both are ignorant of a fundamental reality in the Christian world view, and they are equally erroneous in their claims concerning neutrality.

Finally, and most tragically, the irrelevance of God in the human sciences has set up unnecessary competition between the interpretations of social science and those of the church. Because the objective scientist is compelled to understand aspects of the human condition as if God is irrelevant, traditional insights into the human condition are assumed to be less than scientific (and probably wrong). Conversely, because the findings of social science are always presented in a naturalistic context, many Christians have assumed that the scientific study of humanity is, ipso facto, a threat to their faith.

Take, once again, the case of the "Damascus Road convert." The objective scientist explains the convert's experience as if God is irrelevant to the event, offering a naturalistic explanation rooted in existent social and psychological conditions. The convert denies this scientific explanation because it ignores the premise that his conversion was the result of God's

Spirit working in his life. The one possibility that neither person takes into consideration, however, is that God may be working through social and psychological processes to bring about His will.[8] The objective scientist ignores this possibility, regardless of his or her personal beliefs, because it is an inappropriate scientific conclusion. The convert ignores it because he views it as a secular interpretation of a spiritual event. Both, however, are wrong—the objective scientist, because God is banished from His own creation, and the Christian convert, because God is confined to some sort of "spiritual" domain. As a result, we get neither good science nor good theology—nor a great deal of Christian insight into the human condition.

THE ARROGANT DISCIPLINES

As noted in chapter 4, one of the consequences of objective science was to eliminate the concept of sin and gradually to diminish the significance of human finitude. Thus, the human being as a fallen, limited creature was expunged from the scientific literature. Some objective scientists, of course, continued to think of sin as an important "personal" issue; many philosophers of science continued to debate the problem of error; and most ethicists of science continued to grapple with the issue of scholastic integrity. However, all of these discussions were either assumed to be beyond the scope of objective science (such as the discussion of sin) or readily resolvable within naturalistic categories (such as the problems of error and ethics). As a result, objective science moved methodically in the direction of sinless perfection and its adherents espoused theories that were increasingly arrogant.

Arrogance, of course, is a many-headed monster. For most of us, the term conjures up images of people we have known who tend to be thoroughly self-consumed and aggravatingly self-confident. Those of us in academic circles are especially familiar with such personality types. This conventional form of arrogance, however, is not the issue here. While personal arrogance is a serious malady and far too many scholars fall victim to it, it is a far less epidemic disease than the substantive arrogance characterizing much of modern science. Thus, it is important to keep in mind that when we assert that the product of objective social science is arrogant we are discussing theoretical substance, not personalities. It is the stuff of science—methodology, theoretical conclusions, and applications—that commands our attention at this point, not the character of the practicing scientist.

Method. First, let us explore what I call the arrogance of method. The modern social sciences were founded by people who were firmly convinced that the methods of objective science were profoundly superior to all other ways of knowing about the human condition. This opinion, however, was not merely a preference or ethnocentric bias. It was a conviction based on the assumption that science provided its practitioners with certain or indubitable knowledge—what might be called foundational knowledge. Since other ways of knowing were assumed to be something less than certain (usually *much* less), science was thought to provide at the very least a superior route to truth. More often than not, it was believed to have rendered nonscientific methods obsolete.

August Comte, called the founding father of sociology, provides a good, if somewhat exaggerated, example of methodological arrogance.[9] Comte conceived of societies and knowledge as moving through three developmental stages of growth. The first of these he called the "theological" stage; this was a society whose method of understanding was based upon the belief that God (or supernatural forces) was responsible for all worldly events. In such a society, if one asked why a rock falls to earth, one would receive the response, "Because it is the will of God." According to Comte, science is quite impossible in a society trapped within a theological approach to knowledge.

The second level of societal development was termed the "metaphysical" stage. Here explanations for physical events are derived from the properties of the physical elements themselves. Instead of supernatural forces causing things to happen, events are seen as resulting from their own fundamental essence or nature. An Aristotelian, for example, might say that a rock falls to the earth because it belongs on the ground. That, for Comte, is a good illustration of the kind of thinking that characterizes a society in the metaphysical stage of evolution.

This is superior to theological explanations and contains the possibility of genuine understanding, but it is only a transitional step toward the final objective.

Comte labeled the final rung of the evolutionary ladder the "positive" stage. A society reaching this level is one that seeks to understand things only "as they really are." Its search for truth is based upon neither theological nor metaphysical speculation, but rather a dogged determination to accept only empirical facts. This is a society in which science can flourish and truth prevails. It is the zenith stage of knowledge development.

Readers who have come this far will no doubt be less than impressed with Comte's line of reasoning. Not only is it historically dubious to argue that societies have passed or are passing through such stages of development, but it is also not at all clear that Comte's three "ways of knowing" are either mutually exclusive or exhaustive.[10] Moreover, in retrospect it is evident that Comte's association of positive science with "fact" or "truth" is highly problematic (see the discussion of the problem of certainty in chapter 5).

But for our purposes the important thing about Comte's thinking is not the adequacy of his developmental theory but his assumptions about the nature and position of modern science. Quite clearly, Comte is assuming that modern scientific methodology is not merely a good, helpful, or productive approach to knowledge; it is the *only* sure path to truth. Indeed, he was so confident of this claim that he proposed the idea that societies should be run by an elite group of sociologists. (We should all thank God that the political leaders of nineteenth-century Europe had the good sense to decline Comte's offer!) But before we dismiss Comte as a mere hyperbolic character, we ought to recognize that his suggestion of a ruling elite of sociologists and other scientists is perfectly logical if one assumes that modern science is the ultimate route to truth. Who would be better able to run a society than those who study it by using objective scientific methods and who rely exclusively upon empirical facts? Who, indeed.

Fortunately, most modern social scientists have not been as thoroughly and radically logical as August Comte. In fact,

Comte's work is significant today not because of its substantive merits but because Comte was willing to push the logic of positivism to such an extreme degree. What ought to trouble us about Comte, in my opinion, is that his position does have a great deal of internal validity. If the methodology of objective science is what its adherents claim, then Comte's unabashedly arrogant positivism makes perfectly good sense. Such good sense, however, is not appreciated in an age of political pluralism and social civility. Thus, Comte's logic is usually laughed off today as the excesses of an old eccentric. Laughter, however, regardless of its nullifying intent, cannot mask one rather crucial point. Comte's assumptions about the preeminence of objective scientific methodology remain the mainstay, in function, if not in rhetoric, of contemporary social science. Methodological arrogance in the social sciences today is different from Comte's only in degree—not in kind.

Theory. The advent of objective science, of course, brought about much more than arrogant methodology. It stands to reason that if assumptions about method lack humility, then theoretical conclusions will be similarly predisposed. And, indeed, such is the case.

At the outset, let me say that the form of theoretical arrogance we are interested in here is not an arrogance of style. Many scientists of every persuasion present their theoretical analyses in a rather arrogant fashion. B. F. Skinner, Carl Sagan, and Milton Friedman come readily to mind, though I am sure the reader could come up with a much more personally satisfying list. Regardless of how one evaluates those who present their theoretical conclusions in such a fashion (and I suspect that has something to do with whether or not we agree with their conclusions!), arrogance of style has more to do with the personality of the theoretician than with the substance of the theory. Our concern at this point is not style but substance.

Briefly then, from a Christian perspective, a theory is arrogant if it assumes that God's creation can be explained without reference to the Creator or that apparent problems within the creation can be understood without regard to sin. If one believes that the world and all its inhabitants have their origin in the Creator and that He continues to sustain and to reign sovereignly over His creation, then any theory failing to take that into account not only is highly predisposed to error but also is excessively vain. It purports to be something it cannot be; it pretends to explain something it cannot explain. It is like the virtuoso who claims that his artistic abilities can be understood purely in terms of his own aptitude and genius without regard to the influence of his teacher. Few virtuosos are so arrogant. But such vanity is the stuff of most modern scientific theory.

Similarly, to offer a theoretical explanation for a social problem without regard to sin is also arrogant. If sin is a central human reality, then its presence affects both the social theorist and the social theory. Thus, the theory that excludes sin as a dynamic force in human existence is arrogant about its explanatory capacity. This is so, I might add, regardless of whether the theory presents an optimistic or pessimistic picture of the future of humanity. Christian social scientists sometimes align themselves with pessimistic theories of human behavior because they believe such theories comport well with a biblical notion of sin. That assumption may be false, however. Max Weber's pessimistic predictions about the future of the bureaucratized state[11] and Marx's optimistic vision of a classless society[12] are equally arrogant, for example, because both theories account for future human possibilities without regard to either sin or redemption. This does not mean, of course, that they are equal in substance, since one theory may offer a more accurate view of present conditions than the other.

Application. Pragmatic folk that we are, we may understand the issue of arrogance more readily in the application of a theory than in the theory itself. Arrogant ideas, for some reason, are sometimes more palatable than their behavioral counterparts, so we will consider the arrogance of application before concluding this discussion. To do so, we will examine the lives of two extremely influential social theorists, Herbert Spencer and Karl Marx.

Herbert Spencer was a nineteenth-century English social philosopher. His insights into the nature and dynamics of society were highly influential both in the infant disciplines of anthropology and sociology and in certain segments of British and American politics.[13] Without getting too complicated, let me simply say that Spencer's theory turned on the idea that societies develop very much like biological organisms. Having assumed an evolutionary understanding of organismic development, Spencer hypothesized that societies evolve from simple organizational forms into complex social arrangements. Like its biological counterpart, the societal evolutionary process is guided by a kind of natural selection: the strongest elements within society tend to survive, while those parts unable to accommodate to changing social conditions are eliminated. This notion was sometimes called Social Darwinism, and it implied that social change was naturally progressive and, I might add, self-justifying.

For our purposes, the interesting point about Spencer is the manner in which he applied his theory to the social problems of his day. Because he assumed that a society progressed through the persistence of only its most vigorous elements, he argued that it was regressive to aid the weakest segments of society. He reasoned that by enabling the least fit to survive, a society would actually retard its own development. Thus, for the long-term good of society, the most prudent social policy was one of noninvolvement in the lives of the needy. He asserted that social programs designed to aid the poor were, in fact, harmful to the health of society and should be avoided at all cost. He believed this so strongly that he toured many of the great cities of the West, proclaiming the wonders of social evolution and denouncing those who called for social legislation to help the poor and destitute.

Karl Marx, of course, presents an interesting contrast to Spencer.[14] Though he, too, based his theory of social change upon an evolutionary scheme, it was a theory far removed from the selective mechanisms of Social Darwinism. For Marx, the key that unlocks the mysteries of societal development is class struggle—the inevitable clash between those who control the means of production and those who represent the new forces of production. This conflict, according to Marx, occurs in *every* historical epoch and *always* results in the overthrow of the current ruling elite by the new class.

In our age, the epoch of capitalism, the controlling class is represented by those who own the economic resources and those who do their bidding. They are locked in futile combat with the working class, the latter representing the new forces of production. This conflict between the capitalists and the workers is inescapable because the two classes have opposing interests: The capitalists desire ever larger profits, according to Marx, and these profits must necessarily come at the expense of the employees, in the form of lower wages. Because the capitalists possess both economic and political power, Marx argued that they would inevitably be successful in their quest for greater profits. This success, however, would lead to their own demise. Once the workers realized how thoroughly exploited they were, they would coalesce into a powerful political movement, revolt, and expropriate the economic resources of the bourgeoisie.

Though Marx was convinced that the future he predicted was inescapable, he was not willing simply to sit back and watch it come about. In part, this was because his theory contained the ethical assumption that the capitalists' use of the working class for their own profit was immoral. For the employer to profit from the efforts of the employee was prima facie evidence of exploitation, according to Marx. Moreover, his theory contained the psychological assumption that the overthrow of capitalism would only come about after the workers were fully aware of their exploitation—after they shed their "false consciousness." It therefore became his duty to raise the consciousness of the proletariat—that is, to help the laborers see the "true" nature of their situation. To that end, of course, Marx and his colleagues dedicated themselves. Indeed, Marx was so convinced of the truth of his theoretical analysis that any price was worth paying to bring about the communist revolution, including the use of calculated deception (propaganda) and violence. This, of course, is the now famous doctrine of the ends justifying the means.

For our purposes, the instructive thing about the theories of Spencer and Marx is not the theories themselves but the practical implications of arrogant theory. In both cases, the arrogance of theory gives rise, quite logically, to an arrogance in application.

From a Christian perspective, of course, the theories of Spencer and Marx are profoundly arrogant. This does not mean, remember, that they are stated in an arrogant style, but that they assume to be something they cannot be. In these examples they are arrogant because they feign to offer an explanation for the destiny of human society without taking into account either the existence of a sovereign God or a fallen, finite creation. Thus, they presume to understand human history without regard to the God who charts the course of nations, and they predict a future without regard to sin. In short, their theories assume a position of omniscience unavailable to finite creatures. In purporting to give us a God's-eye view of human fate, they attain the very heights of arrogance.

A theoretical posture of arrogance is not without its consequences. In the case of Spencer, it allowed him to countermand a central tenet within his own cultural tradition—the care and protection of the poor. Even though the concerns of the poor have been much ignored at various times in Western history, a norm of responsibility has been a clear and unequivocal assumption. "Those who have, ought to help those who have not." What is impressive about Spencer's theory, then, is that it is not only able to justify the position of the wealthy—they are the fittest of the survivors—but able as well to turn the vice of selfishness into a virtue. For Spencer, it was altogether altruistic to be niggardly toward the poor since it would foster the progress of society as a whole. To label such a notion "arrogant" is to greatly understate the case. But for those willing to buy into the assumptions of such a theory it is frightfully reasonable as well.

With Marx, one confronts the same kind of logic directed at a very different target. In Spencer's case, it is the needs of the poor that can be rightfully ignored for the greater good of society; for Marx, it is the humanity of the entrepreneurial class that can be safely forgotten. Admittedly, Marx grounds his assumptions in a much more elaborate moral schema than Spencer. He argues, for example, that the termination of the bourgeoisie is not only justified because of the resulting greater good, but also because, as exploiters of the working class, they deserve their fate. The bottom line, nevertheless, remains constant. We are asked to ignore the needs and rights of one segment of humanity in order to bring about some greater good. In other words, we are asked to set aside traditional notions of justice and fair play in order to bring the theorist's concept of a better future to fruition.

It would be hard to imagine a more arrogant request. It assumes, for one thing, that the theorist *knows* the future—that his theory of social change is beyond dispute, that it is the very essence of truth. Moreover, it asks us to believe in a radically new morality—to believe that the theorist's understanding of moral truth ought to supersede all previous moral claims. Gone is the notion of sin. Gone, too, is any concept of human limitation. Gone as well is any evidence of scientific humility, caution, or discernment. Present instead is a new faith, with its own moral edicts and its own vision of human destiny. Present, instead, is a new god.

CONCLUSION: THE NAIVE DISCIPLINES

The god of the early social theorists still lives. He is worshiped a bit differently in the last half of the twentieth century, but he is sovereign nevertheless. Although his devotees are somewhat less arrogant in style and their analyses more focused, they still do their social science as if sin and finitude were inconsequential and as if the God of creation could be safely ignored.

At first glance this may seem an odd assertion. After all, few contemporary social scientists would embrace the claims of a Comte or a Spencer, and even the followers of Marx (though numerous) tend to be much less adamant about their conclusions. Indeed, most modern social scientists—those who write articles that appear in standard professional journals—seem perfectly oblivious to the issues that prompted the passions of the early theorists. So how is it possible to accuse them of falling into their forefathers' footsteps?

The chasm that appears to exist between the early social scientists and their modern counterparts is predicated primarily on one thing: breadth of analysis. The intellectual background of the early theorists allowed them to range broadly in their writings, moving from the philosophical context of their science all the way to its social or political implications. Thus, the substance of their theory, including methodology and possible applications, was never hidden from the reader; its logic and assumptions, as well as its arrogance, were laid out for all the world to see. This breadth of analysis, however, had one significant defect: it consistently led to failure. The futures charted by men such as Comte, Spencer, and Marx simply did not come to pass. Needless to say, such predictive failures threw into question the adequacy of the theorist's vision. As a result, students of the early theorists (and their students' students) increasingly restricted the scope of their analyses, hoping to find safety in the minutiae of human events. Today, therefore, except for a few rather brave souls, we find the social-science landscape littered with millions of highly specialized studies on everything from flossing behavior to postmortems on the personalities of dead presidents.

But though the breadth of analysis has become restricted, what else has changed? Not the theoretical assumptions. The social scientists still remain locked within a closed system of cause and effect. Not their methodological assumptions either; they still reduce the subject to an autonomous objectivity. And not the meaning context of the social scientists' analysis; the data are still interpreted as if they occurred within a transcendent void. The statistical techniques have been refined and the attention to detail has become more consuming. But the fundamental framework has changed little. The object is still to inquire into various aspects of the human condition and to do so in abstraction from its most salient Truth.

And what about success? Has the contemporary social scientist become more successful in reaching his objective? The answer, of course, depends on what one means by "success." If one is interested primarily in the accumulation of specific observations and multivariate correlations, then, of course, there has been more than a measure of success. If, too, one is satisfied with social scientists who pump out vast quantities of (what one must assume are useful) data for governments, media analysts, ideologues, and professional associations, then once again there has been much success. But if one is interested in gaining an understanding of the human condition, then the modern social scientist has, by most accounts, failed miserably.

In the modern social sciences, then, one finds an immense paradox. On the one hand it is a gigantic operation, churning out vast quantities of information; some of these bits of information, moreover, are useful to those who employ them, whether they be bureaucrats, revolutionaries, or parents. On the other hand, the information itself is based on a philosophical context that is explicitly naturalistic and—from a Christian perspective—profoundly arrogant. As a result, rather than leading to a fuller understanding of the human condition, it leads instead to a truncated view of humanity. The irony is that many modern social scientists assume that, because they are amassing great quantities of data, they are ipso facto acquiring a better grasp of the human condition. The tragedy of contemporary social science, therefore, may be that it contains not only the arrogant assumptions of its founding fathers but also a rather large dose of naivete as well.

TOWARD A CHRISTIAN UNDERSTANDING OF HUMAN RELATIONSHIPS

Two propositions are central to all that has been said so far. First, a person's assumptions about truth and ultimate reality affect the way he or she thinks and lives. This is, of course, in no sense deterministic. One cannot predict exactly an individual's ideology or lifestyle, for example, simply by knowing the assumptions held by that person. The influence of assumptions, however, is profound and consequential; they reach into every corner of our lives with an impact that is both visible and significant.

We also have explored the effect of assumptions on science, initially by examining the role of Christian assumptions in the early development of modern science and then by analyzing the consequences of the shift from Christian to naturalistic assumptions. We finished that section with an investigation into the problems associated with naturalistic presuppositions in science and with a discussion of the ramifications of such assumptions for the development of the social sciences. Our conclusion—and second proposition—was that modern social science is both rooted in and suffering from the consequences of naturalistic thinking: that it is naive, arrogant, and something less than Christian.

These two propositions lead, I believe, to the conclusion that a Christian perspective in the social sciences is both proper and necessary. It is proper because assumptions about the ultimate nature of reality are unavoidable. They must be made, and are made, in the social sciences just as elsewhere. Like the naturalist, the Christian has the legitimate right to approach science from the vantage point of a specific world-and-life view.

For the Christian, however, such a perspective is not only legitimate, it is also necessary. It is necessary, first, because integrity demands it. To call oneself Christian is to affirm that Jesus Christ is Lord. And from His Lordship no area of life can be safely excluded. It is necessary, second, because the social sciences are in need of Christian thinking. Without it, these disciplines will be less than they should be and the world will be deprived of a source of understanding it both needs and deserves.

It would be a dreadful mistake, however, if one concluded from our analysis that Christians can now confidently ignore the insights of modern social science. The discovery that the social sciences are naturalistic ought to improve our vision, not make us blind. All humanity shares the benefits of common grace, including the world of the naturalistically inclined scholar. Christian social scientists, therefore, will want to grapple with, benefit from, and sort through the insights of naturalistic science. But one cannot sort through unless one has a position to sort from. For the Christian scholar, that means a position rooted in biblical thinking.

THE PRACTICE OF SOCIAL SCIENCE WITHIN A CHRISTIAN CONTEXT

It is, of course, one thing to proclaim the need for Christian scholarship; it is quite another to fill the need. Christians have always been adept at telling one another they ought to be more thoroughly Christian, whether in business, neighborhood, or science. We have been less skillful, however, at actually being the kind of people we exhort others to be—at actually being Christian businessmen, Christian neighbors, and Christian scientists. "Practice what you preach" is a well-worn phrase— and with good reason.

We are better at the preaching than the practicing because the former entails far fewer risks. The one who exhorts us to be good neighbors, for example, may be labeled preachy, boring, or a poor scholar, but few will quibble with his message. Indeed, if he articulates the sermon well, he may be venerated and richly rewarded. Those who actually try to be good neighbors, however, rarely receive such earthly plaudits. More likely, they are scorned as do-gooders, meddlesome busybod-ies, or psychologically maladjusted bleeding-hearts. For every acclaimed Mother Theresa there are hundreds of others who die, unknown and undecorated, amid the impoverished they sought to serve.

And yet the purpose of exhortation is not the production of better preachers but of better practitioners. It is at the doing that the sermon is aimed; it is by their actions that the faithful are known. And while to have the good-neighbor message is preferable to no message at all, it is better still to have a good neighbor.

The first part of this book was something of an exhortation. It was an attempt to argue the merits of Christian scholarship in the social sciences and to encourage fellow travelers to think Christianly about their subjects. What this means, I suspect, is that I have completed the *easy* part of the task. Granted, arguing the case for Christian social science is, in the present context, a bit more arduous than making a plea for neighborliness. The latter, fortunately, is still considered a virtue in the modern world; the former is not. Regardless of the formidability of the task, once done it is still nothing more than a call to action—a bald assertion that Christian scholarship should and can be done.

The second half of this book attempts to rectify that deficiency. Our focus will move away from the issue of legitimacy toward the problem of practice. The question will shift from "whether" it should be done to "how" it might be accomplished. Specifically how does one go about the project of thinking biblically about the subject matter of the social sciences—that is, of doing social science within a Christian context?

For at least two reasons, this is a difficult question. First, there is the problem of contemporary Christian thought. In general, twentieth-century Western Christians do not know how to think Christianly about most subjects. We have reduced Christianity to a matter of morality and have ignored the broader implications of the biblical imperative. As a result, when Christians are asked to think biblically about a social issue, they invariable translate "biblical" into "moral" categories and turn the discussion into a discourse on social ethics. While the moral claims of Christianity are extremely important and not to be ignored, any approach to social science that is exclusively moralistic will be gravely deficient. Indeed, it will not be science at all. To engage in a Christian understanding of the social sciences, therefore, requires a much grander concept of God than is currently held by many Christians.

Second, there exists the problem of contemporary scientific thought, which is almost entirely naturalistic and, from a Christian perspective, reductionistic. This, of course, is the problem discussed at some length in the first portion of this book and there is no need for further detail here. The difficulty, however, is that the naturalistic perspective so dominates contemporary science that even many Christians have difficulty conceiving a Christian alternative. Such Christians tend to see the worlds of science and Christianity as mutually exclusive domains, the former having to do with nature and the latter with matters of the spirit. For them, the worlds of science and Christianity are so inherently at odds that any attempt at reconciliation leads almost immediately to various states of apoplexy.

Like the moralistic Christians, these "spiritual" Christians have a very limited image of God. Safely ensconced in the domain of the spiritual and supernatural, such a god is not about to enter the sphere of nature. To bring such a god into the realm of an empirical science, then, is a difficult, almost impossible task. Indeed, it requires an image of God unheard of in many Christian circles—the Author of Salvation must become the sovereign Lord of Creation as well.

Once these problems are resolved, the task of Christian scholarship may become less formidable, but the question still remains: How shall we engage in a Christian understanding of the subject matter of the social sciences? That is the question of the hour. To deal with it, I want to take up a topic that concerns most social scientists to some degree: human relationships. I will develop a framework for the study of human relationships that, I trust, is consistent with a biblical picture of God's world and that will serve as an example of how Christians might approach other topics within the social sciences. Let me stress, however, the illustrative nature of this task. No one should conclude that I am proposing *the* Christian framework to gain *the* Christian understanding of human relationships. Rather, I hope to have developed *a* Christian framework in order to gain some insight into *a* particular topic. The framework was chosen because it was the one that seemed most reasonable to me. The topic of human relationships was selected because of its general interest to a wide variety of social scientists and also because it is a subject in which as a sociologist I have some degree of expertise.

THREE ESSENTIAL ELEMENTS

A Christian investigation of any subject within the social sciences should, I believe, be composed of three elements. First, a Christian philosophy of science needs to be articulated to provide biblical guidelines and parameters for the Christian social scientist. Second, a biblical understanding of the subject under investigation must be developed. And third, the study itself needs to take place within the context of the Christian assumptions established under the first two points. A primary implication of this approach is that questions about the ultimate nature of reality (relative to both scientific method and the subject) must be raised and tentatively resolved *before* the scientific investigation takes place. Unless such an approach is used, the modern researcher is doomed, by default, to employ the assumptions of a naturalistic world view. The decision to do that, however, must not be made by default but through careful deliberation. This is especially true for the social scientist who claims to be Christian.[1]

If we are to engage in a Christian understanding of human relationships, therefore, we must begin by articulating a philosophy of science that is consistent with a biblical picture of the world. How should the Christian social scientist view his task? What should he assume about himself, the world he studies, and the results of his investigation? These, of course, are the questions we addressed in chapters 3 and 4 about the value of God's creation, humanity's responsibility to under-stand and watch over it, the "type of world" God created, the "nature of the being(s)" we are, and the constraints implied in God's greatness, human finitude, and sin. While there is no need to repeat these assumptions at this point, I wish to stress that I believe they are crucial to a Christian approach to science. The history of modern science informs us that slight modifications in some of these assumptions (e.g., the "type of world" assumptions) and the elimination of others (e.g., the "Christian constraints") spawned a naturalistic version of science quite different from the original. If nothing else, such a scenario ought to make us conscious of the importance of developing an explicitly Christian, thoroughly understood, philosophy of science.

The second element of a Christian approach to the social sciences ought to be a biblical understanding of the subject matter. That means, in our case, that we must develop a biblical appreciation of the nature of "human relationships." Who are we as relational creatures? What does Scripture have to say about human relationships—with God, one another, and the rest of creation? How does our relational nature affect our behavior? These are just a few of the questions we will seek to address in the next chapter as we attempt to gain a biblical understanding of the human condition in its relational context.

The final element of a Christian social scientific perspective is the application of this framework of biblical assumptions to the study of a particular human phenomenon. In a real sense, this is the "doing" of social science. Here the focus shifts from how we *ought* to see to the actual process of seeing. This is the world of scientific discovery. As every social scientist knows, the task of discovery is a multifaceted one, running the gamut from metatheoretical paradigm construction to meticulous, painstaking observation. Since our objective is to develop a biblical framework for the study of human relationships, our analysis will of necessity be restricted to the broader, more theoretical level. A Christian social science, however, is by no means exclusively theoretical in content. Indeed, the Christian social scientist ought to be profoundly interested in the details of human activity. What follows in chapters 8 through 12 is largely theoretical, not because I lack interest in empirical observation, but because my efforts have only just begun.

Chapter 7

ON THE HUMAN CONDITION: THE RELATIONAL CONTEXT

Attempting to lay out a definitive statement, however modest, of what the Bible has to say about anything is fraught with difficulties. There are all the usual problems of interpretation and possible error as well as the problem of selectivity. Where do we look, for example, when we seek to discover biblical assumptions about human relationships? My guess is that this question has resulted in as much disagreement among Christians as has the broader hermeneutical issue.

To develop a Christian understanding of any aspect of the human condition, I believe one must begin with the large picture as the Christian community has tended to see that picture over the years. In other words, the quest should start with a grasp of central biblical truths in a way that is consistent with the historical interpretations of the church. I say this not simply because I wish to be as inclusive as possible (though I do). Rather, and more importantly, I believe that we will be in grave danger if we begin our journey by addressing issues that are too specific. The latter could both generate needless internal controversy and lead to substantial error. One *must* interpret specifics in the light of the whole. An out-of-context biblical interpretation is not a biblical interpretation at all. And we will not get anything like a Christian social scientific perspective out of it.

In this chapter, then, we will focus on some of the principal claims of Scripture concerning the human condition, especially its relational aspects. They are largely contained in the Genesis account and they ought to be familiar to anyone who has had some exposure to Holy Scripture. Their familiarity, however, should not lull us to sleep. For I am convinced that they are teeming with implications for the student of the social sciences.

THE RELATIONAL GIVEN

The first biblical insight we must come to grips with if we are to pursue an alternative social science is this: God created the human as a *social* being. God designed the human being to be a relational creature. Note this point well. Humankind was created to relate to other beings. It was not an accident. It was not the result of sin. It was an intentional, creational given.

God. The first dimension of this relationship, of course, is the human being's communion with God. "In the beginning God created."[1] That fact alone implies a relationship between God and all of His creation. But a very special relationship is established with one part of that creation: human beings, made in the image of the Creator. God poured Himself into humanity in a unique way, giving human beings both the opportunity of direct communion with Him as well as the possibility of making a relational choice with regard to the Creator. This is an important point, I believe. The nonhuman creation was designed to be in a certain relationship with God and was offered no choice in the matter. But when God created the human being He established a volitional relationship, one that involved the will of the creature.

A few comments about humanity's relationship with God may be helpful. First, the fact that God established a volitional relationship with human beings does not mean that human beings were allowed to operate willy-nilly as they chose, without regard to God's purposes. It is clear that with the ability to choose came the necessity of living with the consequences of choices made. How the human being responded to God, therefore, was of great consequence, affecting future choices and constraining humanity's volitional character.

Second, humanity's relationship with God was predicated upon certain responsibilities. Adam and Eve were told to "fill the earth," to "subdue" and have "dominion" over it, to "till and keep" the Garden, and not to eat fruit from the "tree of the knowledge of good and evil."[2] All of these requirements implied that God's relationship with humanity was set within a certain order. For our purposes, then, it is important to remember that *human beings were designed to relate to God in a certain way;* humankind has a constitutional need to be so related.

Finally, the fact that God created human beings in His image implies certain social characteristics. From the very outset, the Bible presents God as a relational being. He has a court full of angels, for example, and there seems to be no end to His multitudes of "heavenly hosts." Moreover, Christians believe in the Trinity—that God is, in and of Himself, a social being (Father, Son, and Holy Spirit), both one and three at the same time. All of this suggests that God's character is relational in essence and that those whom He created in His image will be relational by design.

Humanity. The second relational given recorded in Scripture concerns the relationship between human beings. "The LORD God said, 'It is not good that the man should be alone; I will make him a helper fit for him.'"[3]

This rather amazing statement by God indicates, once again, His concern with companionship. When God made this statement, we must remember, man already had a relationship with God. Immediately thereafter, moreover, all of God's creatures were brought before Adam, but still no suitable companion could be found. Thus, the Genesis account teaches that neither relationships with God nor relationships with non-human creatures are enough to satisfy the relational need He put into the heart of humanity. The human being needs other human beings.

And so, Eve was created. She came, in a sense, to complete God's creation, to eradicate the possibility of loneliness, and to finish the creation of humanity ("male and female he created them"). By this I am not suggesting that men are somehow incomplete without wives or that women are incomplete without husbands; the Bible makes it quite clear that marriage is not a prerequisite for human fulfillment. It does mean, however, that human beings were created to relate to one another in a social context and that this is what God intended for humanity. Aloneness *is not* good for human beings; togetherness *is* good for human beings. Companionship, it must be understood, is the intended creational norm.

I am aware that I am being somewhat repetitious on this point, but for one reason or another we seem to need to be reminded that we are social beings. Like many others in our society, Christians sometimes emphasize the individual over and above the human family. For Protestants in general, this may come from an emphasis on individual choice and religious freedom. For evangelical Protestants, it may be due to the stress placed on the individual's need for salvation. For others, it may simply result from the influence of Western individualistic values. Whatever the cause, there is nothing biblical about a picture of humanity that is ultimately individualistic. The *essential* (ultimate, fundamental, or whatever) character of humanity is social.

Creation. Finally, God's plan assumed a certain relationship between humanity and the rest of God's creation. We have already mentioned that God told Adam and Eve to till the Garden and to subdue and have dominion over the earth. This seems to suggest a threefold relationship with creation.

First, it indicates that humanity was given authority over God's creation. This not only means that human beings can exercise their will with regard to nature but that they are clearly of greater value to God. The pantheist or the naturalist who identifies humanity totally with nature is wrong. Human beings are different. They are more significant and they are more precious.

Second, however, though human beings are of more value than the rest of God's creation, their authority over the earth is delegated authority. Human beings did not create the earth; God did. And God gave humanity the responsibility of taking care of His creation. This stewardship function does not mean that humankind can do anything it chooses with creation. We are managers, taking care of the King's property, and we shall be held accountable for our actions. In short, humanity's authority over the earth is not unlimited or unconstrained. It implies responsibility.

Finally, human beings were expected to subdue the earth. In the context of authority and stewardship, this indicates that we are both to use God's world and to bring it under our control. I take this to mean that the world is not only available to us but that it is our responsibility to exercise authority over it. When we till the ground, domesticate an animal, or learn about the wonders of God's creation, we are fulfilling our creational responsibility before God. It is a good thing. We ought to rejoice and be glad in it.

THE RELATIONAL PROBLEM

We see, then, that we were created to be relational beings. Human life on earth was set in the context of communion with God, companionship with one another, and stewardly authority over God's creation. It would be nice if that were the end of the story. But it is not.

I noted earlier that God created the human as a volitional being, a creature with the ability to make relational decisions. One choice we are all profoundly aware of was the choice of disobedience. Humanity decided to reject God's creational plan in favor of one of its own. This, of course, is what we call the Fall, and it ushered humanity into the era of sin.

There were, certainly, many consequences of the Fall. Theologians have talked about them at great length. We are not interested in pursuing each of these consequences here. Rather, we will focus on what can be called the relational effects of the Fall. That is, how did sin affect God's intended relational order?

God. The most significant consequence of the Fall is that it came between God and His human creation. In a very real sense, it severed the communion intended by God. Obviously, this does not mean that human beings could no longer communicate with God or that there was no longer a context for a relationship. But it does mean that God's relationship with humankind was significantly altered by sin and that the intimacy and totality of the created relationship was now missing.

The record of the Fall in Genesis 3 is instructive. The first words of God after Adam and Eve's disobedience came in the form of a question to Adam; He simply said, "Where are you?"[5] As a question, this is somewhat peculiar, since God certainly knew where Adam was located. But as a statement, it is most profound. For suddenly, with sin, there is difficulty in communication. It is a problem generated by the attempt of Adam and Eve to hide themselves "from the presence of the LORD God"[6] and acknowledged by God in the form of a question. Both God and the Garden dwellers immediately recognized that they had a relational problem: they had become estranged from God through disobedience.

The symbols of estrangement in the Genesis account are numerous and blatant. First, Adam and Eve hide from God. Second, Adam proclaims a new-found fear of God. Third, he recognizes his "nakedness" before God. Fourth, God must expel Adam and Eve from the Garden (a garden He created just for them; there is a sense of great pathos here). And fifth, we find that human beings will return to the dust from which they were created.[7] These are not mere suggestions that something is amiss. They indicate, rather, that the intended relational order was radically altered by sin and that discord and alienation now characterize the relationship of God to His special creation.

Humanity. We often concentrate on the effects of sin within the vertical context—and for good reason. However, we do sin a great disservice if we ignore its consequences for relationships among human beings. Here too we find that the Bible is not quiet.

In basic terms, the Fall had the same alienating effect upon human relationships as it had on the relationship with God. Once again, God's intended relational order was shattered, altering drastically the mode of human interaction. We see this illustrated in the Genesis account of God's conversation with Adam immediately after the Fall and in the curse placed on Eve.

When God confronted Adam with the question, "Have you eaten of the tree of which I commanded you not to eat?"[8] Adam responded by blaming the woman for his disobedience. The response, though a familiar one, is revealing. Suddenly the man is willing to sever the relationship with the woman—a relationship that was created as a remedy for his aloneness—in order to shield himself from blame. That Adam really thought such an excuse would work seems unlikely, given his knowledge of the character of God. Whatever he may have thought, the fact that he was willing to try such a pathetic ploy suggests his state of desperation at the time as well as a new-found contempt for the value of human companionship.

The curse that God placed on Eve also indicates a relational problem. "To the woman he said, 'I will greatly multiply your pain in childbearing; in pain you shall bring forth children, yet your desire shall be for your husband, and he shall rule over you.' "[9] Note the relational issues involved with the curse: First, pain will accompany the establishment of a family; second, "desire" will replace giving as a basis for the marriage relationship; and third, "rule" will replace oneness in companionship. In other words, with sin we move away from human relationships based upon the fulfillment of mutual needs— primarily the need for togetherness—and toward relationships designed to satisfy personal wants. It is a move from "we" to "I." It should be pointed out as well that this new state of affairs was neither what God wanted originally nor what He desires for us now. The curse represents a condition that humans have fallen into as a result of sin; it most certainly *is not* a biblical standard for godly relationships.

In both of these examples, we see that, with the Fall, relationships that were once complete now become strained and difficult to maintain. Human beings become alienated creatures—alienated not only from God but also from one another. Sin struck at the heart of humanity's need for companionship.

Creation. Finally, sin also affected humankind's relationship with the rest of God's creation. To Adam, God said "cursed is the ground because of you; in toil you shall eat of it all the days of your life; thorns and thistles it shall bring forth to you; and you shall eat the plants of the field. In the sweat of your face you shall eat bread till you return to the ground."[10]

What we see here, of course, is the further erosion of God's original relational plan for humanity. Although God intended for human beings to have full dominion over creation, authority now must be exercised with great difficulty and some measure of pain. And while God initially desired stewardship responsibilities to be fulfilling and enjoyable, now those same tasks are laced with "thorns, thistles, and sweat." Work becomes redefined and humanity's relationship with creation is now measured by pain as well as joy. In short, the sin that produced alienated relationships with God and other human beings also brought about humanity's alienation from creation.

THE RELATIONAL DILEMMA

When one puts together all we have just considered—the way God created His world (the relational given) and the way humanity altered His design through disobedience (the relational problem)—one is confronted with a genuinely pathetic picture. It is a picture of humanity in the predicament of its life. We will call it "the relational dilemma."

On the one hand, we were created in such a way that we can only be fully human in the context of God-given relationships. The Bible makes it clear that, simply by virtue of how God created us, we have a certain need to be related to God, to one another, and to the rest of God's creation. I call this a "need," in spite of the difficulties this term has experienced in the social sciences, because I want to stress that relationships are not an option for us. They are rather a given—a part of our very essence, the way we were created. We are social beings and we *need* relationships.

On the other hand, we are also fallen creatures. And because of the Fall, we find ourselves estranged and alienated. This means that our essential need for relationships is to a large degree thwarted. The Fall left us incomplete and unfulfilled. It left us with an aching need to be related but without the knowledge or tools to fully satisfy that need. Moreover, as we will see, it put humanity on a desperate journey to satisfy this relational void.

Before going on to look at the implications of this predicament, it is important to understand that the "relational given" and the "relational problem" constitute a genuine dilemma. Much philosophy and theology, it would appear, seems dedicated to the task of resolving that dilemma by focusing upon either Creation or the Fall. Thus, we find ourselves wading through myopic discourses which argue in favor of human potential (and ignore sin) or human depravity (and ignore creation). But these approaches simply will not do. Human beings are neither essentially "good" nor "bad." We are created/fallen beings with a social need and a relational dilemma.

The resolution of this dilemma, therefore, cannot be accomplished by human effort, either by focusing upon Creation or the Fall: it rests solely in the hands of the Creator. If one is a Christian, of course, one believes that God has devised a plan for such a resolution and that He did so from the very beginning. Indeed, it would not be an exaggeration to say that the Bible is, in part, a record of God's efforts to deal with the relational dilemma. It shows, for example, that God—because He is a God of mercy, love, compassion, and grace—has consistently reached out to reconcile His creation to Himself. Jesus Christ is the culmination of that reconciliation process. He is the bridge by which humanity is being, and will ultimately be, reunited with God and all of God's creation.

But the biblical record is not only about God's reconciling activity; it is also a story about the attempts of men and women since the Fall to resolve the relational dilemma *on their own terms;* to satisfy their need for a relationship with God and with others by means other than those devised by the Creator. This, of course, is the story of sin. And neither it, nor creation, nor the story of God's efforts at reconciliation can be ignored if we are to attempt the construction of a Christian approach to human relationships.

Chapter 8

SUBSTITUTION:
THE CASE OF IDOLATRY

It is my conviction that the relational dilemma provides a context for a Christian understanding of social life. The statement of this dilemma in the preceding chapter does not in any way exhaust biblical insight for such a task. But I do believe that the relational dilemma incorporates a number of crucial biblical assumptions about the human condition, assumptions that should be accounted for in a Christian approach to the social sciences. Assuming this to be the case, what are the implications of the relational dilemma for the study of human relationships? That question will provide the framework for the remaining portion of this book.

Our starting point is the assumption that human beings have an inherent need to resolve the relational dilemma. Since humans were created as relational beings (the relational given), and since humans are alienated from their intended relational objects (the relational problem), their present situation is marked by a need to relieve the tension caused by the conflict between these two conditions. The significant question for us, therefore, is, How does mankind go about trying to resolve the relational dilemma?

RESOLUTION BY SUBSTITUTION

The most obvious method of dealing with any kind of alienation is through an attempt to reestablish the broken relationship. If the bond of trust between husband and wife is broken, for example, reconciliation usually takes place when both partners accept responsibility for the problem and seek to mend the relationship. Thus, one way of handling estrangement is to resurrect the original relationship.

The "original" relationship in humanity's case, however, is that which exists with God, and the reason for the existence of alienation is human sin. Thus, this is not a mutual *falling out* between two parties of equal status. It is a situation in which the created being, fully knowing the consequences of the act, willfully disobeyed the Creator. Therefore, any reestablishment of the relationship is dependent solely upon the will, and one might add mercy, of the Creator. This means that for humanity to become reengaged with God, it must do so on God's terms. Unfortunately, human beings find that a very difficult pill to swallow. Consequently, they repeatedly attempt to alleviate their sense of alienation by entering into illegitimate relationships. I call such attempts "resolution by substitution."

The table on the following page illustrates the various relational possibilities between human beings and the objects of their relationships: God, other human beings ("Humanity"), and the rest of God's creation ("Creation"). The horizontal rows represent the potential objects of a particular relationship, while the columns indicate how one might relate to these objects. For example, if a person related to God's creation as if it were God, the result would be creational idolatry (box a). Humanistic idolatry (box b) would be an attempt to relate to other human beings as if they were God; and so on.

The table illustrates that humans may try to remedy alienation through a variety of relationships. Most important, alienation may be reduced by an attempt to build relationships based on biblical norms: that is, we may relate to God as God (c), humanity as humanity (e), and creation as creation (g). Human beings can come to God *on God's terms* in order to reestablish relationships, not only with the Creator but also with humanity and the remainder of creation. The biblical record and the witness of the church indicate that God has provided the means for such renewed relationships through the death and resurrection of our Lord and Savior, Christ Jesus.

ATTEMPTS TO RESOLVE THE RELATIONAL DILEMMA THROUGH SUBSTITUTION

		The Object Treated As		
		God	Humanity	Creation
The Object	Creation	(a) creational idolatry	(d) creational humanism	(g) *normative*
The Object	Humanity	(b) humanistic idolatry	(e) *normative*	(h) humanistic utilitarianism
The Object	God	(c) *normative*	(f) theological humanism	(i) theological utilitarianism

Before proceeding to the other types of relationships, two comments need to be made concerning biblically normative relationships, boxes c, e, and g. First, the fact that someone accepts God's standards for renewed relationships does not necessarily bring about such relationships. The Bible indicates that redeemed people continue to sin and thus fall prey to the seduction of illegitimate relationships. However, it does mean that the ultimate relationship with God has been reestablished permanently and that the potential exists for entering into relationships on the basis of the "relational given." This potential derives from the Christian's access to God's Spirit, His Word, and Christ's church.

Second, the normative categories (c, e, and g) are important because they represent biblical criteria for human relationships. These norms represent the way things should be—the relational givens which God established within the essence of His creation. Since we touched briefly on their content in chapter 7, I will not repeat that here. Suffice it to say that these criteria are the standards by which relationships must be judged and are at the core of any Christian understanding of human relationships.

CREATIONAL IDOLATRY

When we move beyond these biblical standards, however, we enter the realm of illegitimate relationships. These are ways in which people try to resolve the relational dilemma on their own terms without reference to God's relational givens. The methodology, of course, is simple substitution. On the surface, such a strategy seems quite peculiar. Why would anyone want to substitute a false relationship for the genuine article? After closer analysis, however, we find such attempts neither surprising nor rare.

"Creational idolatry" (box a) is a case in point. Strange as it may seem, history is replete with humanity's efforts to satisfy the need for God through relationships with God's creation. Over and over again, we find that the creational "things" which God has given us for our enjoyment and use—things that should point us to Him—have been transformed into the means by which we attempt to satisfy our need for Him. We turn the creation into a god.

This process is not strange at all. It is, rather, quite familiar and somewhat predictable. The first step seems to occur when, personally or vicariously, we experience something good, such as the acquisition of knowledge or the feeling of physical pleasure. We define the experience as good because it *is* good; God made it that way. Then, because we enjoy such an experience, we desire to have it again and again. In time, we decide the good experience is worthy of all-out pursuit. As we pursue it, the "thing" quickly becomes the object of our adoration and love. It becomes a god. But it is not God and so, of course, it never fully satisfies. Sometimes we recognize this fact and reject the false god (particularly if we get satiated with it), sometimes we do not (usually when we are less successful at reaching the objective). It makes little difference, however, since normally we replace one false god with another anyway. And thus, life becomes an exercise in flitting from one false promise to the next.

The thing to notice about creational idolatry is that it is not merely a theological observation. When people treat created things as worthy of divine adoration, they are engaging in a profoundly human activity. This has significant implications for the social scientist. The fact that we tend to think otherwise indicates our tendency to overly compartmentalize knowledge—especially "religious knowledge." Such thinking, however, implies a sacred/secular distinction that is certainly less than biblical. Its roots are similar to those that produced "objective science."

In Western industrial societies, the most readily discernible form of creational idolatry is that behavior which we find associated with consumerism.[1] This is the rather blatant display of what can only be described as material worship. One hour of American television, for example, contains a host of consumer appeals, all absolutely dripping with the idea that some "thing" (car, home, athletic events, toothpaste, even religion) can bring deep personal satisfaction and ultimate fulfillment. Moreover, the fact that some people laugh at the ridiculousness of such appeals should in no way deter us from recognizing their significance. One only has to watch those same people promenading through town in a new car to know that the message of the advertisement struck a responsive cord deep in the heart of the consumer.

It should be apparent that consumerism, as an expression of creational idolatry, is not simply an economic phenomenon. It is found in the whole range of human experience. It serves as an illusory form of ultimate fulfillment. The self becomes convinced that its identity can be bolstered by the acquisition of material goods. Thus, worth is measured by possessions and one's estimate of personal value is based upon one's belongings. Creational idolatry is not only fundamentally wrong, but it also leads to two significant personal problems. On the one hand, for those who define themselves as materially successful, creational idolatry becomes a balm against deeper dissatisfaction. It protects them from their genuine need for God.[2] On the other hand, for those who think of themselves as material failures, creational idolatry leads to a false sense of their own worthlessness. They feel depreciated and of little value.

From this perspective, *both* self-confidence and self-abasement can be problems if rooted in creational idolatry. Such a conclusion, obviously, flies in the face of much modern therapeutic theory which assumes that mental health is subjectively defined by the patient. Thus, the person who suffers from depression and a deep sense of worthlessness is perceived as having a problem, while the self-confident achiever is not. Volumes of psychoanalytic and pseudopsychoanalytic literature (probably more of the latter) are produced each year relating to problems of depression, identity crises, insecurity, etc. Almost nothing is published exploring the problem of self-assurance, positive thinking, or self-reliance.[3] The reason is clear. In our world it is almost inconceivable that such things could be thought of as problems. People in hot pursuit of materialistically defined prestige are not about to shell out dollars to be told that their chosen route to happiness is fundamentally flawed. But it is. And a Christian understanding of creational idolatry ought to confront us with that fact.

Relating to God's creation as if it were God has social ramifications as well. When ultimate loyalty is given to things, our behavior accommodates our desires, and we shape society accordingly. Political institutions, for example, are likely to protect property over human interests, since the former is of central concern. Because political power is often held by only a few in any given society, this can mean that laws and ordinances will be designed to protect the material interests of the political elite.

Religious institutions can feel the sting of creational

idolatry as well. At the very least, if they attempt to point people away from purely material interests, they find their job much more difficult—they lose a certain degree of social legitimacy. More likely, however, since religious institutions are not immune from the values of society, they will become increasingly inclined toward a material definition of their own success (e.g., the size of churches, programs, budgets, etc.). This can lead to religious institutions that are materialistically successful but religiously superfluous.

Other examples are possible, but central to our concern is simply that a population devoted to material worship will suffer the effects of its own devotion. In other words, creational idolatry will have empirical consequences. It seems to me, therefore, that one of the tasks of the Christian social scientist would be to explore the relationship between this form of idolatry and the psychological, political, economic, and social conditions of society.

If, for example, consumerism in modern societies is a form of creational idolatry, then it cannot be explained purely in terms of "market forces" or "repressed sexuality" or "class conflict"—though all of these may describe an aspect of the issue. Rather, the origin and force of consumerism lies in an attempt to satisfy the need for God—in this case, in an attempt by the West to relate to creation as if it were God. To miss that point is to miss a crucial issue in the development of Western industrial societies. Yet it remains an unexplored point in the social sciences, not only because it would be considered inappropriate in some quarters, but because it is antithetical to the assumptions of a naturalistically rooted science.

Obviously, my assertion of the relationship of creational idolatry to Western consumerism is theoretical and in need of a well developed argument if it is to be at all persuasive. Such is clearly beyond the scope of this document. The significant issue, however, is that, from a Christian perspective, people do choose to substitute aspects of creation for God and to relate to creation as God. This *is* an empirically salient fact. It will affect in some very concrete ways the lives of the people who make such a substitutionary choice.

HUMANISTIC IDOLATRY

The idolatrous relationship is not limited to the material spectrum. For just as things may be substituted for God, so may other human beings. We may thus attempt to resolve the relational dilemma by relating to humanity, or aspects of humanity, as if it were God.

In a sense, humanistic idolatry is more subtle than creational idolatry. Creation, in God's plan, was never intended to be loved (appreciated, yes; loved, no). Therefore, acts of love directed toward creation are fairly easy to discern. Human beings, however, *were* created to love one another with all the affection, compassion, and charity they can muster. For this reason, the human heart that replaces love for God with love for people (or a person) is not always easily spotted. Nevertheless, substitutionary devotion is no less pathological when it comes in the form of human adoration. Indeed, one might argue that its ability to masquerade as the real thing makes it even more problematic.

Humanistic idolatry can be divided into two types, the first focusing on human beings per se, the second on derivations of human relationships, namely, social forms. In the former, individuals attempt to relieve their alienation from God by entering into human relationships in order to find ultimate fulfillment. Once again, our society is full of examples. In particular, the romantic relationship is presented not only as a locus of mutual love and affection but as an avenue to final fulfillment and satisfaction.

As I pen these words, I am listening to a song that graphically illustrates this problem. The singer is Neil Diamond and the song is "The Shelter of Your Arms." Both the artist and the composer paint a vivid picture of a man in the midst of great turmoil and misery who finds a haven in the arms of his lover. Indeed, the man's lover provides him with the only compelling reason to live.

Here is a beautiful, deeply moving song—I stopped writing to listen to it—that tells the story of a profoundly idolatrous relationship. For clearly, the ultimate frame of reference for this man—his security, strength, safety, and shelter—is his love relationship with another human being. He has found his god in the arms of his lover. But she is not God and his relationship with her is doomed to failure because it cannot possibly live up to his expectations.[4]

Romance, however, is not the only repository of humanistic idolatry in our society. It can also be discovered in parent-child relationships, where the parent finds ultimate fulfillment in the vicarious joy of a successful child; in religious organizations, where multitudes worship at the feet of some great guru, or evangelist, or pontiff; in sporting events, where millions put their faith in the physical prowess of an athlete; or in politics, where would-be presidents promise omniscient leadership.

Such forms of humanistic idolatry are not without their consequences. Psychologically, the inevitability of failure contained in such relationships either dooms the participant to despair and depression or to an endless search for a relationship that will finally satisfy (a kind of manic-depressive psychosis). Sociologically, the endless search tends to undermine the development of long-term relationships, particularly in the voluntaristic atmosphere of modern pluralistic societies. As a result, fragile, easily threatened relationships are threatened further still by expectations they cannot possibly meet. Such relational instability can only lead to reduced social solidarity within the society and a loss of "rootedness" or sense of belonging for its inhabitants.

The objects of humanistic idolatry need not be limited to other human beings, however; social forms may also become victims. In this case, a social form—such as government, family, or even religion—can become the relational substitute for God. Simply put, one begins to relate to the social form as if it were one's ultimate frame of reference. For example, when the family is used in this manner, one's life begins to revolve exclusively around family values. The family becomes the focal point for decisions relating to time, priorities, money, whatever. Thus the family, which is certainly a good thing, can squeeze out other obligations—to neighbor, community, government, religion, etc. (*also* very good things). In my opinion, middle-class America, in which I confess membership, suffers a great deal from this malady.

Government and one's involvement in politics can also be the source of ultimate fulfillment. This seems particularly likely in societies where problems are generally defined in political terms with assumed political causes and solutions.[5] This leads to the same "squeeze-out" phenomenon earlier attributed to the family. It also gives the political sector a large measure of power and influence, encouraging the penetration of political means into every area of life and possibly setting the stage for an extreme form of totalitarianism. It is a phenomenon, once again, not without empirical consequences.

Chapter 9

SUBSTITUTION: THE CASES OF HUMANISM AND UTILITARIANISM

CREATIONAL HUMANISM

Returning to the table in chapter 8 (p. 109), we move to the first box under the heading "Humanity" (box d). Here we confront the possibility of relating to creation as if it were human. This does not necessarily mean that interpersonal relationships are replaced with relationships to elements of creation (although it could; the hermit is a good example of this). It does indicate, however, that creational relationships are elevated to a level equal to that of human interaction and that the meaning of creation is established in terms of the meaning of humanity. Though this may sound mysterious, it is nothing of the sort. Two examples—one from politics and one from natural science—may serve as illustrations.

Like many other things we have discussed, the concern for ecology is a good thing. As stewards of God's world, we need to be concerned about technological innovations that threaten the quality or survival of creation. However, the rhetoric of the ecology movement often indicates that more is going on than mere stewardly concern. In its extreme form, this rhetoric implies that nature (creation) has a *right* to be left alone—to be unspoiled by the designs of human beings. Certainly all of

God's creation ought to be protected from abuse and exploitation. And certainly some portions of that creation ought to be
preserved for human enjoyment. But it is not true that nature
has an inalienable *right* to be left alone. Such a statement is
blatant anthropomorphism and indicates that creation has
taken on human qualities.

Similar types of anthropomorphic innuendo periodically
emerge from the mouths of naturalistic scientists, especially
those burdened with the task of explaining the origins and
development of life. Typically, the crucial term is "nature," a
word pregnant with human overtones. Within this genre, we
learn that nature makes "decisions" about survival, "guides"
the selection of species, and generally "directs" the evolutionary process. Though we plebes are never provided with a
precise definition of this thing called nature, it is clearly
something of vast human potential, with a personality of its
own. And though we all surmise that the scientist does not
really believe in "nature," we also understand that the modern
scientist would be lost without it.[1]

While both of these examples testify to the existence of
creational humanism in modern industrial societies, its social
impact is also found in cultures that are less advanced
technologically. Here anthropological data suggests that people
often relate to creation as if it were inhabited by divine spirits
(creational idolatry) or as if it were inhabited by some form of
human, possibly ancestral, spirits[2] (creational humanism) or by
some combination of the two. The social significance of this
type of creational humanism is that it tends to inhibit the
development of technological innovations which might serve to
improve the general well-being of the community. This occurs
because creation presents itself to the people as a "brother"
with the same rights of freedom from undue infringement that
human beings possess.[3] Consequently, nontraditional uses of
creation not perceived as bearing on the immediate survival
needs of the community are greatly discouraged.

Having said this, I am aware that my comments may sound
somewhat ethnocentric to those schooled in the values of
cultural relativism. I trust that such is not the case. Please note
that I am not assuming that some forms of technological

development (e.g., Western capitalism) are superior to others or that Western technological radicalism is preferable to the technological conservatism found in other societies. Actually I think there are relational problems with both positions. I am asserting, however, that creation was given by God for us to use and enjoy through wise stewardship; that those cultures that relate to creation as a brother are doing so incorrectly; and that such incorrect relationships will hinder people in those cultures from fully exploring the possible uses of creation for both their betterment and their pleasure.

THEOLOGICAL HUMANISM

The possibility of relating to God as if He were human will be termed "theological humanism." It indicates that God can be reduced to the level of humanity and that human beings can, in their effort to resolve the relational dilemma, pretend that God is merely "one of us." It is an interesting, if troubling, possibility. And, unfortunately, it is one to which Protestant Christians seem particularly predisposed.

The problem seems to result from an exaggerated emphasis upon Christ's humanity, as opposed to His divinity, as well as from a rather superficial understanding of God's forgiveness (e.g., "cheap grace"). Obviously, an analysis of this problem is far beyond the bounds of this treatise. Suffice it to say that I believe that these are erroneous positions, inconsistent with some of the core relational assumptions of the biblical record. Protestants are right in emphasizing the humanness of the historical Jesus; they are wrong in ignoring the fact that He was and is God incarnate.[4] Likewise, Christians—Protestant and otherwise—are correct in proclaiming the salvation that God has offered human beings through the blood of the Lamb; they are incorrect, however, when they lift this event out of the context of God's justice.[5] Christ became the Son of Man not in order to change the essential character of either God or humanity but to bridge the gulf created by sin and to offer a genuine resolution of humanity's relational dilemma.

The existence of this erroneous view among Christians is in itself quite instructive. It shows that even those with access to

Scripture and the teachings of the church can be conned into the use of illegitimate means to resolve the relational dilemma. The pain of alienation is intense; and those who fail to employ God's solution, whether they have knowledge of it or not, will be driven to remedy the ache in other ways.

Though theological humanism is, as its name suggests, a theological problem, it nevertheless has some rather intriguing empirical implications, especially for the field of study known as the sociology of religion. In particular, the growth of theological humanism can lead to the development of a religious ideology that does not provide a basis for transcendent judgment. When God is reduced to a "buddy" or mere friend (though He may be a friend, He is not *just* a friend), He loses His authority to be Judge and holy, righteous Other (two qualities Christ never gave up during His earthly sojourn). This means, of course, that the god of the theological humanist does not have the ability to be morally prophetic. For this reason, even though the advocates of theological humanism may make moral proclamations, these generally have very little impact. Devoid of both ideological legitimacy and transcendent authority, such proclamations are unlikely to move the church to prophetic action.[6]

As far as sociological implications, then, one might expect that a religious organization operating on the basis of theological humanism would, over time, lose its legitimacy as a real moral authority, and thus its general societal influence would be eroded. This does not mean that it will immediately lose its popularity. Both Christian conservatives selling pop psychology and liberals selling cheap grace have found moments of ecstasy riding the wave of theological humanism. In the long run, nevertheless, its influence should wane. To put it bluntly, why should one go through the machinations of purchasing pop psychology or cheap grace in religious form when one can buy the straight stuff much less expensively elsewhere?[7]

HUMANISTIC UTILITARIANISM

As God can be reduced to the level of humanity, so human beings can be reduced to the level of creation. Thus, there are times when we attempt to handle our estrangement from others by relating to them as if they were merely an aspect of God's creation. I have called this effort to pluck the image of God out of the hearts of men and women "humanistic utilitarianism."

Unfortunately, examples of this kind of relational phenomena are all too prevalent. We have already discussed the inherent tendency of naturalistic science to treat humanity and creation monolithically; this can be done by way of "creational humanism" or "humanistic utilitarianism." The latter seems most problematic from a human standpoint, however, because it approaches humanity with the same kind of detached, manipulative objectivity that is usually reserved for nature. The ethical vacuum implied in this approach is, I think, rather disturbing. From a Christian perspective, it is also wrong. The relational givens set forth in the act of creation indicate that we are to relate to humanity and nature differently. This is just as true in science as anywhere else.

The world political scene also provides evidence of humanistic utilitarianism. For example, note the similarity between this relational predisposition and the rationale for political terrorism. Hostage taking, executions, and acts of violence all are justified in terms of some political objective—with high and noble ideals, no doubt. As a result, human beings are used as pawns in a game of political influence. The striking thing about such activity, however, is not its mere existence, but the fact that it is so readily understood by modern man. We moderns have no difficulty comprehending the possibility of equating human beings with property, to be used as barter in a political dispute. We laugh, by contrast, with incredulity at the medieval concept of a joust, where, theoretically, kingdoms were sometimes won and lost on the outcome of a carefully conceived and agreed upon contest between two individuals. Our comprehending of the former and our incredulity at the latter speak, one suspects, of the influence of humanistic utilitarianism in the modern world.

The social significance of this relational assumption is multidimensional. First, to the extent that social patterns depend at least partly upon shared moral values (though the influence of coercion cannot be ignored), humanistic utilitarianism is socially disruptive. This would only cease to be true in a community of complete totalitarianism, in which case humanistic utilitarianism would be the modus operandi and social patterns would be maintained by force rather than moral legitimacy.

Second, assuming a society with a moral referent of some kind, the intrusion of humanistic utilitarianism into any segment of the society would lead to a shift from obligatory to coercive relationships. In the economic realm, for example, one would expect that relationships based on mutual responsibility and trust (e.g., consumer trust in product claims and business responsibility to back up its claims) would be replaced by patterns of interaction that assume avarice and deception (e.g., consumer greed and caveat emptor). This same shift from moral obligation to coercion might occur in the relationships of the neighborhood, the school, and even the family. In other words, inevitably there is a drift away from genuine humanitarian concern and compassion.

Finally, self-concepts must also be adjusted to the demands of humanistic utilitarianism. One cannot relate to others as things, to be used as means to an end, without recognizing the implications of such thinking for oneself. I too must become a thing, available for manipulation and abuse. I too am of value purely in terms of my utility to others (for my beauty, intelligence, power, wealth, etc.). I too am of no ultimate significance. Clearly, a society with a population bent on resolving the relational dilemma through humanistic utilitarianism must bear a heavy psychological burden.

THEOLOGICAL UTILITARIANISM

We come to the last feat of substitution, the possibility of attempting to relate to God as if He were creation. This may seem a bit strange. How can one possibly try to use God as if He were a mere object of nature? And even if one attempts such an effort, of what empirical import can it be for the social scientist? Both questions are important to address. And since the answer to the former is more apparent than the latter, we will begin with it.

To understand theological utilitarianism, it might be helpful to dust off an old anthropology text and look for a functional
definition of "religion" and "magic." In one way or another,
"religion" will be defined as behavior directed toward some
transcendent reality as an end in itself, while "magic" will be
described as the attempt to use that transcendent reality as a
means to achieve some material goal. This functional definition
of magic, regardless of whether or not it is indeed "functional,"
is a good description of theological utilitarianism.[8] For here the
human being attempts to use God for his own purposes as if
God were a Valentine's Day card, a pep pill, or a sledge
hammer.

When seen in this light, one will note that magic is not the
exclusive possession of so-called religious primitives. It rears its
head whenever religious leaders seek to use the one they
worship for their own purposes. The magicians are sometimes
evangelists, with neat formulas for instant happiness; sometimes faith healers with quick cures for painful and debilitating
conditions; sometimes prophets with simplistic answers to
complex political and social problems; and sometimes priests
with mysterious techniques for organizational growth and
power. Whatever the form, the result is the same: The religious
leader is lifted up and God is brought low.

The socially significant element in all of this, I suspect, is
deception. For the God of creation is not creation and He
cannot be manipulated. What can be manipulated, of course, is
truth and the fears and hopes of seeking people. The task of
religious leaders so inclined, therefore, is to convince the
faithful that they have exclusive access to the power of God, to
be used as they see fit. Because this is a task that demands
deception, it leads to the development of a religion filled with
secrets, magic, and mysterious ritual. And its success is directly
related to the ignorance of the flock.

As religious organizations based upon theological utilitarianism grow or as religious groups move in this direction, a
number of things will begin to occur (assuming a modern,
pluralistic context). First, power will increasingly be vested in
the religious leader. This happens both because of the leader's
exclusive access to and use of God and because the leader must

maintain control over the mystery of his or her own power. Second, to assure the leader's authority and to safeguard secrets, an increasingly authoritarian power structure must be designed, one that is heavy on obedience and light on servant-leadership. Third, both the charisma of the leader and the efficiency of the authoritarian organization will tend to produce growth and a successful recruitment effort. Finally, to borrow a term from Erving Goffman, the religious organization will increasingly resemble a "total institution," demanding more and more of the parishioners' time and resources.[9] The last point is important because it means that this kind of religious organization tends to usurp the functions and responsibilities of other social institutions (e.g., family, government, etc.).

Obviously, this analysis of the effects of theological utilitarianism is intended to be illustrative, not exhaustive, and we cannot fully explore the ramifications of this fascinating but tragic phenomenon. Remember that illegitimate relationships not only fail to satisfy but they can be cruel and dangerous. Not a few of those seeking a relationship with God have been seduced by the purveyors of theological utilitarianism; not one has found it there.

CONCLUSION

In the last two chapters, we have taken a look at the relational dilemma in an attempt to understand some of the ways people try to resolve it. I have argued that one mode of coping with alienation is through substitution: replacing God-intended relationships with illegitimate ones. After specifying a number of different types of substitutionary possibilities, I have attempted to discuss their significance as well as implications for the social scientist. Substitution, however, is not the only avenue that can be used in an attempt to resolve the relational dilemma, and in the next three chapters we will investigate another approach: The attempt at resolution through denial.

Chapter 10

DENIAL AND ULTIMATE REALITY

As we approach the topic of denial, we should keep in mind the meaning of the relational dilemma. It results, fundamentally, from the estrangement that sin brought into the heart of human affairs. This alienation, however, exists in the context of the relational given, which means that in spite of our alienated condition we nevertheless need to be related because that is how God created us. Thus, we have a problem—a relational dilemma. It raises the following question: How do people deal with the tension caused by the inherent conflict between this relational need and their condition of alienation?

This question is particularly troubling when we focus on the ultimate context—our relationship with God. One way to deal with the problem is to affirm the biblical norms established for the relationship. In that case, we would relate to God as Creator and understand ourselves as created beings. The problem here, however, is that, unless we deal with the issue of sin, we will find it extremely difficult to live within the biblical norms. Because of this, the relational dilemma is more often addressed through illegitimate means. One option, which we have already discussed, is resolution through substitution. Another option, our point of departure in the next three chapters, is resolution through denial. This involves an attempt to eradicate the relational dilemma by denying the creational status of one party involved in the relationship. In the case of our relationship with ultimate reality, denial can involve either God or humanity.

HUMANISM: DENIAL OF THE TRANSCENDENT

One possible attempt at resolution, therefore, can be made by simply denying the existence (or influence on human affairs) of God or any transcendent reality. I have termed such an approach "humanism," not because I think transcendent denial constitutes an appropriate definition of humanism or because I enjoy using humanism as a whipping boy but because it seems to me that a central assumption of modern humanism is the denial of either the existence or importance of God.[1] It sees human beings as fully responsible for their own fates and believes that God-dependency is a genuinely harmful human characteristic. For the humanist, atheism or agnosticism is a positive platform to use as a basis for living life. This is also the position of denial.

Using the humanist label would be unfortunate, however, if it blinded us to the existence of forms of denial outside the rubric of traditional humanism. Indeed, the tendency toward humanistic resolution has been with us for some time—the Book of Genesis is full of examples[2]—and it often presents itself in religious costume.

The Judeo-Christian tradition has been particularly adept at incorporating this tendency. Theologically, it emanates from a quite correct concern for human responsibility, stewardship, and a rejection of moral despair. But the seduction of humanistic denial seems so strong that Jews and Christians are forever proclaiming that "the future is in our hands," without reference to God, His will, or His sovereignty. Protestants became vulnerable to this form of denial when they appropriated a humanistic concept of reason and attempted to use it as a basis for Christianity; this all but eliminated the need for faith in one's approach to God or to human understanding.[3]

We have also discussed the influence of humanistic denial in the development of science. While the growth of naturalistic science represents the cruder form of this tendency, the story of objective science is also one of humanistic denial. It essentially assumes that one can engage in scientific understanding without reference to God. Indeed, in both science and religion, the fundamental modern assumption seems to be that the task at hand can be accomplished more effectively if one ignores the existence of God altogether. This is the assumption of the "God is dead" theology; it is the assumption of objective science; and it is the assumption of a humanistic denial.

FATALISM: DENIAL OF HUMANITY

The relationship between God and humanity, however, can be denied without ignoring the influence or existence of God. Rather clever folk that we are, we have also come upon the idea of affirming God but denying humanity. This approach, called fatalistic denial, allows us to transcend the relational dilemma altogether by emphasizing either the control or the pervasiveness of God, thereby eliminating the relational tension.

The most obvious form of this type of denial can be found in the assumptions of pantheism. Here the oneness of all things is assumed and that oneness or unity represents God. Human beings as separate, created beings do not exist. The goal for the pantheist, therefore, is to transcend humanness and to become conscious of unity with God. Engaging in this effort, one quickly loses any sense of sin, human pain, human responsibility, and (the pantheist hopes) any sense of a relational dilemma as well.

A more subtle form of fatalistic denial occurs whenever we give up our fate—whether to the wind, the gods, or anything else. Not accepting responsibility for one's past or one's future is a denial of the biblical picture of humanity. It ignores the fact that at creation God gave human beings the responsibility of doing certain things (e.g., stewardly tasks). We were also created with the need to make certain choices (e.g., obedience versus disobedience). To deny these creational givens is to deny an aspect of our humanity.

History—and, I suspect, the personal experience of each

one of us—is loaded with examples of this type of fatalism. Sartre called it "bad faith"—the notion that life presents itself to us with no real choices.[4]

"I don't want to become a soldier, but I am being drafted, so what choice do I have?"

"I didn't mean to cheat, but I couldn't help myself!"

"I'm falling in love again."

All of these statements assume events over which we have no control. But, as Sartre contends, that is bad faith because it denies the possibility of saying no, regardless of the consequences. The potential soldier may be put in jail, but he or she can say no; the student may flunk the exam, but she can say no; the romantic may lose a lover, but he can say no. We all have options available to us, whether we acknowledge them or not. Most important for our discussion, however, is that we fail to acknowledge these options because they confront us with the relational dilemma. Through fatalism we attempt to absolve ourselves of responsibility before God. It implies that our sin is uncontrollable and therefore not of our own doing; it seeks to reduce relational tension by denying an aspect of the person God created.

IMPLICATIONS

For the social scientist, a crucial point emerges out of our analysis of humanistic and fatalistic denial. In the absence of biblical norms to guide the relationship between humanity and God, we can expect knowledge of ultimate reality to move in either a fatalistic or humanistic direction. This insight is relevant both to the philosophy and application of social scientific inquiry.

Philosophical Implications. Anyone at all familiar with social science theory or the philosophy of science will know that an interminable debate is going on about the issues of freedom and determinism. Those holding to the freedom position ("choicism") believe that human beings exercise some degree of free choice in the development of their lifestyles. They say we are free to make real choices that affect our future. Those holding to the determinism position, on the other hand, argue that all our decisions result from prior experiences (social, psychological, genetic, etc.), which in effect determine the decisions we make. Our choices are not free but determined by prior events. In the social sciences, this issue is sometimes reduced to a debate about whether knowledge (ideas, beliefs) can affect social conditions or whether the social context determines knowledge (though we must add that the determinists can handle either option within their framework).[5]

Regardless of the side one takes in this debate (and there appear to be Christians on both sides), one is confronted with significant problems. The determinist faces the problem of meaning and purpose. "If my actions and thoughts are determined, why should I be concerned about this particular issue or about any other? What is the purpose or consequence of my caring?" While religious determinists may impute such a purpose to God, they must still face the implication that they are mere puppets in the hands of forces over which they have no control. Those advocating freedom of choice face the problem of cognitive dissonance. All day long, as human scientists, they do nothing but try to demonstrate how perfectly predictable people are. How do they wed their deterministic, scientific minds with their freedom-loving hearts? The task is difficult indeed.

My purpose in presenting this debate is to point out that it is essentially a form of the humanist-fatalist dilemma. As such, both choicism and determinism represent denials of an aspect of God's relational order. Let us take a closer look.

The choicists contend that human beings are free to make some, or all, decisions. Many Christians agree with this position because they believe humans must be free to choose between obedience and disobedience, between God or the Evil One. Thus, they reject determinism as simply not Christian. But the problem with choicism is that it imputes an attribute of God—free will—to humanity. Only God makes something out of nothing, and only God is "free" to make decisions. God did create humankind as decision-making beings, but the human beings' choices are in no sense "free." They are fully constrained by the way God created humanity, not to mention by the choices of those who have gone before. To argue otherwise, I believe, is to become party to the humanist denial.

On the other hand, when the determinists hypothesize that the thoughts and actions of human beings are determined by prior conditioning, they are engaging in fatalistic denial. They are denying responsibility for their own fates, shifting the responsibility instead to material conditions—or in the case of Christians, to God—over which they have no influence. But surely this denies an aspect of our God-given humanity. We are obligated to make real choices (which are *not* free), and we are expected to exercise God-given responsibilities. Christians who argue that we are determined in the sense that we are optionless beings or mere robots are accepting the fatalistic horn of the relational dilemma.

For this reason, I think it is important for the Christian social scientist to respectfully demur any invitation to become a part of the determinist-choicist debate. It presents two options, neither of which is consistent with the biblical picture of humanity. Moreover, to enter the debate on either side is not only to adopt erroneous assumptions but also to enter into an absolutely futile dispute. Both positions represent an attempt to grab hold of one aspect of God's creation while denying another, and to apply it as if it were the whole truth. But it is not. And thus, any *consistent* application always turns into a quagmire and a paradox. I believe it is a quagmire that Christian social scientists—and, for that matter, theologians[6]—should not step into.[7]

Empirical Implications. To appreciate the empirical significance of denial in the context of ultimate reality, let us return to the principle of denial developed earlier: that in the absence of biblical norms we can expect knowledge of ultimate reality to move in either a fatalistic or humanistic direction. We will see how this principle might apply in the area of sociology with which I am most familiar, the sociology of religion.

From the very beginning, sociologists have been interested in the developmental aspects of religion. Weber and Durkheim, for example, conceived of this as an evolutionary process, though they approached the issue from different perspectives.[8] While I would shy away from using the term evolution at this point, largely because it tends to be interpreted in a deterministic framework, it does seem that the principle of denial implies certain developmental tendencies within religious knowledge. In particular, it suggests that as human beings seek to establish the meaning of ultimate reality outside of biblical norms, they will attempt either to remove the transcendent from worldly involvement or to permeate the world with transcendent reality. This observation seems somewhat obvious until we discover that the sociological community has been almost totally absorbed with only the first of these two possibilities, the one commonly referred to as "secularization."

From a Christian perspective, two things are striking about the concept of secularization.[9] First, it incorporates a rather exclusive definition of religion, one that assumes that only those who believe in the supernatural (e.g., God) are religious. That fact is not particularly bothersome as long as we understand that *religion* here is being divorced from the notion of world view and ultimate meaning. For while people may not be religious in the sense of believing in the supernatural, everyone nevertheless holds to some sort of a world view (a set of ultimate assumptions about the way the world is). Unfortunately, sociologists, as well as many historians and philosophers, sometimes ignore that distinction and thus assume that secularization implies the demise of faith in any concept of ultimate reality. But it does not and cannot. Secularization may be used to suggest the diminution of the significance of the supernatural within one's world view, but not the demise of the world view itself.

Second, if secularization is understood as a tendency within the relational dilemma (humanistic denial), it can no longer be viewed as an inexorable force. Instead, it is simply one of two ways of attempting to use denial to deal with the problem of alienation. It may well be that humanistic denial, or secularization, is the form of denial most likely to dominate a pluralistic society. However, it is by no means the only possibility or even an inevitability. Indeed, pluralistic societies can be ripe breeding grounds for new religious movements (which secularization theorists understand) that represent an extreme form of fatalistic denial and provide the basis for a sacralizing trend (which secularization theorists *do not* understand) and the possibility of "depluralization." Since the history of religion is replete with such phenomena, it is a possibility well worth understanding.[10]

Christianity, it would appear, has been susceptible to both forms of denial. Roman Catholicism, for example, particularly its medieval caricature, seemed to creep into the realm of fatalistic denial. This occurs whenever God becomes indistinguishable from social institutions and cultural patterns and whenever the church engages in the imposition of God upon the total life of the individual.[11] This tendency denies both the humanity of God's creatures as well as their responsibility to exercise discretion in social and cultural matters.

Protestantism, on the other hand, has been more inclined to exhibit the tendency of humanistic denial, though elements of fatalistic denial are also discernible. Liberal theology has often been the carrier of the former; in an attempt to emphasize social responsibility, liberals have sometimes denied any involvement on God's part. Fundamentalism, on the other hand, has sometimes championed the latter; in an attempt to emphasize God's personal involvement in the life of the believer, fundamentalists have at times ignored creational responsibilities. Both examples indicate a departure from biblical norms and, I would suggest, a lack of awareness concerning the meaning of the Atonement.

CONCLUSION

The point, of course, is that denial in the ultimate context is not simply a personal problem, of concern only to God and the individual sinner. It is a problem that affects whole societies, having an impact on the way the people live, think, and worship. People dominated by humanistic denial will live differently than those encumbered by fatalistic denial; both will live differently than those who relate to God as Creator and affirm God's image in His human creation. The social scientist who ignores such differences does so to his own detriment— and the detriment of his science.

But denial affects more than just the object of the social scientist's inquiry. It also delimits the way theorists perceive their subjects. As we have seen, social scientists caught in this dilemma will be tempted to approach their subjects from either a deterministic or choicist perspective. Such a perspective, moreover, will influence the content of their theories, as it has with secularization theorists, predisposing them toward certain interpretations and away from others. For the social scientist, the relational dilemma is not a matter of taste; it is a matter of truth.

Chapter 11

DENIAL AND
HUMAN RELATIONSHIPS

Denial is not limited to the arena of ultimate reality. It can also be observed in the context of human relationships. This form of denial occurs because sin not only estranged humanity from God but also caused a significant rift between human beings (as discussed in chapter 7). The essential problem, therefore, is that any attempt to establish human relationships on a proper (creational) basis without dealing with sin only reenforces the reality of alienation. When we attempt to reduce alienation illegitimately—without addressing the question of sin—we tend to move to one of two extremes. Either we deny our need for others, leading to individualism, or we deny our need for personal identity, leading to communalism.

INDIVIDUALISM

To deny the need for others is to deny an aspect of the way God created us. We noted earlier that God created humans as relational beings, who need and ought to need companionship with one another. When we proclaim, therefore, that we can cope "on our own" and that others should do the same, our proclamation is not only futile but also deceptive.

If this is true, why do human beings keep pursuing

individualism? What makes it appealing? The answer, I suspect, lies in an equation of pain and power. The maxim goes something like this: to the degree one can successfully internalize the philosophy of individualism, one can reduce relational pain and maximize personal power. These two ingredients always seem to go together. If I do not need others, I have thereby insulated myself from the possibility of rejection, and therefore others cannot hurt me. If I can decrease my dependence on others, I can exercise greater control over my own life for I then become free to implement my will more effectively. Unfortunately, along the way I will also give up a portion of my humanity and the ability to enjoy or appreciate God's created order.

Individualism comes to us in many guises. Sometimes it plays on our need for identity and personal recognition, as in Frank Sinatra's proud, if musically flawed, rendition of "I Did It My Way."

At other times it appeals to our insecurity and desire for self-preservation, for example, the idea that "you've got to look out for number one." In the economic realm, individualism often makes the promise that if everyone personally maximizes consumption and profit, the end result will benefit all.[1] In religious circles, it suggests that piety is a private matter between the individual and God and has no business intruding in the public arena.[2] And in the context of politics there is the incessant call to freedom: freedom from other nations, freedom from government regulations (particularly in *my* domain), freedom from taxes (especially those that subsidize social programs for others and make them dependent upon government), freedom from anyone and everyone who is intent upon limiting my freedom.[3] New Hampshire license plates state it bluntly: "Live free or die." "Live free *and* die," however, would be closer to the truth.

COMMUNALISM

Those who live in the West, particularly in North America, find the melody of individualism quite familiar. For some, no doubt, the previous paragraph may have caused more than an occasional wince of incredulity. If so, I trust that the urge to use this book to temporarily solve the energy problem will be suppressed. Clearly there is more to the relational dilemma than the libertarian slogans of a nineteenth-century liberal.

While the critics of individualism among us make some good points, their outcries often mask a different form of denial. It is neither new, as they sometimes claim, nor legitimate, as they always claim. Probably the oldest method of denying the humanity of God's creation is through communalism, a method that affirms the right of the community to squelch the individual if the latter is not perceived to further the interests of the former.

The "community" that perpetuates communalism does not have to be a tribe or fiefdom, however. It can be a nation, culture, race, class, or even the family. Sometimes it takes the shape of "humanistic idolatry," when the social form is substituted for God and the community becomes the ultimate frame of reference (see chapter 9). Other times it is nothing more than pure denial—a ruthless attempt to root out any evidence of personal identity or uniqueness. More often than not, however, it involves a combination of substitution and denial.

Examples of communalism are not difficult to discover. The most famous contemporary expression, of course, is Marxism. Here "class" is substituted as the ultimate frame of reference and the person is useful or important only to the extent that "it" serves the communalistic cause.[4] The oft-quoted (and misunderstood) phrase "the end justifies the means" is among other things a proclamation of the superiority of the claims of the community over the specific interests of the person. All of this, of course, is justified in terms of deep, compassionate, and possibly sincere, concern for underprivileged classes and the common good. But to the extent that the common good legitimates the dehumanization of creatures bearing God's image, it forfeits all claim to goodness.

The political left, however, is not in exclusive possession of communalism. As Adolf Hitler made us all aware, the right is also adept at proclaiming the superior value of the community. Indeed, it would appear that one of the greatest threats to a biblical concept of humanity is nationalism—the attempt to convince the population of any geopolitical community that their interests are best served by forfeiting their personal identities in favor of the collective identity of the nation-state. This is the taproot of much modern patriotism and is the power behind some forms of racism (itself a form of communalism) and ethnocentrism. The slogan "America—love it or leave it," a reaction against the protest movements during the Vietnam War, was not merely an expression of frustration. It was also a rather blunt ultimatum, allowing no room for personal dissent. It might just as well have proclaimed "Nationalism—worship it or face the consequences."

One final comment. Though I have discussed communalism and individualism as contrasting tendencies, it should be noted that they are often integrated in everyday life. The bellicose patriot who defends America as the "land of the free"; the middle-class individualist who dresses, talks, and lives precisely like every other middle-class individualist; the union organizer who carefully guards his right to free speech while collectivizing labor—all of these mix elements of individualism and communalism. This "mixed metaphor" has, of course, been noticed before, usually by those with a communalistic bent.[5] They tend to see it as individualism gone berserk: a mysterious and ironic twist of fate that turns individuality into uniformity, freedom into monolithic conformity. But from my perspective, it indicates neither mystery nor irony but the simple presence of two sides of a single coin. Both are attempts to deny humanity's alienation from itself—to seek resolution of the relational dilemma by repressing essential needs within God's human creation. Sin never demands consistency, only service.

IMPLICATIONS

On the basis of the above analysis, the following principle may be derived: *In the absence of biblical norms, relationships between human beings at both the micro and macro levels will exhibit communalistic and individualistic tendencies of denial.* Since sociologists have historically addressed themselves to this issue, and because they have done so under a wide assortment of labels, I will devote the remaining portion of this chapter to the sociological implications of this principle. The discussion will begin with a brief review of three sociological attempts to understand the phenomenon.

Gemeinschaft und Gesellschaft was not only the title of a book written by Ferdinand Toennies, it was also one of the initial sociological attempts to distinguish between traditional community and modern society.[6] By *gemeinschaft* (literally translated "community") Toennies meant to describe relationships based upon "essential will," an inherent drive to come to grips with one's environment. According to the author, it is particularly endemic to traditional communities and to relationships found in family, neighborhood, village, and friendship groups. *Gesellschaft* ("society"), on the other hand, is an expression of "arbitrary will": a deliberate, purposeful form of behavior oriented toward the attainment of future goals. It is found more readily in modern society and describes what we might call a rational or businesslike relationship. For Toennies it was significant that with industrialization *gemeinschaft* must give way to *gesellschaft* because the values of the latter are the backbone of industrial society—a fact with which he was not altogether pleased. Similar typologies and analyses have been proffered by Redfield (folk-urban), Riesman (tradition, inner-, and other-directed), Durkheim (mechanical-organic), Weber (rational-traditional), and others.[7]

A second distinction worth noting is suggested by the terms "alienation" and "anomie," particularly as discussed by Peter Berger in *The Sacred Canopy*.[8] While Marx and Durkheim ought to receive credit for providing these terms with their contemporary connotations (though Calvin was probably the first to employ the term "alienation"), it is Berger who has provided us with the greatest understanding of their sociological meaning. Far from describing similar phenomena, as many authors seem to assume, Berger stresses that alienation represents a gulf between the individual and his social world, not because it lacks meaning or coherence but because it is something over which he has no control. Anomie, on the other hand, describes a situation in which the individual perceives his social world to be nothing more than the product of his own creation; it has no meaning or external significance because it is merely what he makes of it. Anomie occurs when the norms are in doubt because they have no ultimate legitimation. Alienation occurs because the norms are so massively real that they seem impervious and unalterable. Important to Berger is the insight that these two conditions plague different types of societies. Alienation is the bane of the highly religious (and traditional) society, for the social world is so thoroughly permeated by supernatural meaning that the individual appears to be nothing more than a pawn in its hand. Anomie, however, is the privileged guest of modern secular society. This is because modern society's pluralistic condition allows for virtually no agreed-upon legitimation and thus its norms seem meaningless and groundless to its inhabitants. Though Berger seems to prefer anomie to alienation, his numerous writings indicate that he is profoundly concerned about anomic effects within both religion and the larger society.

Finally, I want to note briefly that sociological theorists have tended to characterize modern society in two contradictory fashions. The first, particularly popular in the fifties and early sixties, described societal elements in functional terms. It emphasized that out of the competitive nature of industrial society came a kind of functional balance and order, each competing element recognizing the functional necessity of the other.[9] Sociologists of another color, popular in the sixties and seventies and appropriately called conflict theorists, saw nothing functional about this competitive struggle at all. Rather, they perceived that industrial society rested on the conflicting interests of different social groups—that one group's gain was another's loss, and the freedom of one class, another's repression. For them, modern society was inherently unstable, imbalanced, and usually unjust.[10]

For our purposes, the significance of each of these distinctions is that they all represent forms of individualistic and communalistic denial. Despite the varied foci of their analyses, and despite the different theoretical frameworks of the authors—among them a German rationalist, a phenomenologist, numerous functionalists, and neo-Marxists—they have nevertheless plucked their sociological insights from the same tree. A few like what they have found, but most are profoundly disturbed. Why?

Those in the disquieted category would include Toennies, Berger, and a segment of the conflict theorists, especially those conflict theorists who perceive conflict to be a "nature of man" problem. Though their orientations are different, they all are in a similar predicament. For Toennies, the problem is a loss of community which occurs in the transition from *gemeinschaft* (communalism) to *gesellschaft* (individualism). Though contemporary sociologists disagree on this point, it seems to me that Toennies was personally concerned about the breakdown of traditional relationships which accompanied the onslaught of *gesellschaft*. In other words, he was worried about the victory of individualism over communalism.[11] For Berger, the disquiet resembles a Catch-22. Traditional society provides the individual with the security of a "sacred canopy" but also the oppression of a monolithic, alienating social structure (communalism). On the other hand, its inevitable replacement, modernity, offers the individual the joys of freedom and choice, but also the agony of *too many* choices and the loss of meaning that accompanies them (individualism). Finally, for those conflict theorists not wedded to a communalistic ideological base, the problem is that industrial society is inherently pathological. It is structured as a zero-sum game, and it cannot be otherwise (that is, modern society is *by its very nature* individualistic and thus conflict-ridden and repressive).

Less melancholy are the functionalists and neo-Marxian conflict theorists. The former are convinced that the competing interests of the industrial society produce a healthy balance. To them, individualism is a positive force. Their only concern is that communalistically inclined regulators will destroy the necessary competition. The latter, while appalled at the inherent conflict within modern capitalism, believe they have a plan (communalism) that can rescue technology from the hands of the capitalists and thereby place modern society on a noncompetitive base. While functionalists and neo-Marxists are both adept at pointing to the flaws of the other, they are altogether myopic about their own.

Essential and Derived Problematics. Clearly, within these three theoretical arguments there exists a good bit of confusion as well as error. From a Christian perspective, this results from a failure to understand the basic nature of the problem. More specifically, I believe that it stems from a failure to differentiate between essential and derived problematics.

The essential problem is the relational dilemma—the absolute, ongoing struggle between our alienated condition and our relational needs. The derived problems, in this case, are individualism and communalism, attempts at denial that represent illegitimate efforts to deal with the essential problem. *Gemeinschaft, gesellschaft,* alienation, anomie, functionalism, and conflict theory all represent attempts to understand and critique elements of the derived problem. Unfortunately, their advocates have mistaken derived for essential problematics, resulting in significant difficulties.

The functionalists correctly perceive the problem of communalism: it achieves order at the expense of personal identity. However, because they see this to be an essential problem rather than one derived from the relational dilemma, they have embraced its alternative—individualism. They have done this because it protects against loss of individuality. However, they also recognize that individualism has a tendency toward conflict. The most ingenious element of functionalism is that it takes this potentially pathological tendency and transforms it into a means for general order and the common good. For this reason, functionalists are sometimes called "order theorists" because they have the uncanny ability to proclaim "order, order" when there is no order.

The neo-Marxian conflict theorists are not convinced by the functionalists' proclamation. They correctly perceive that it sometimes serves to mask individualism's proclivity toward conflict and injustice (the latter occurs because, in an open forum, individualism tends to reward those people and groups with the most power). However, the conflict theorists have defined conflict as an essential rather than derived problem and have thereby found their home in the warm embrace of Marxian communalism. They too recognize that communalism has a tendency toward personal repression. Therefore, using the same magic wand employed by the functionalists, they assert that true identity can only be found in the midst of a classless community. Like the functionalists' claim that out of conflict we get order, this is a half-truth that covers a whole lie.

For Toennies, Berger, and the remaining conflict theorists, the results are not as deceptive but every bit as problematic. All of them, for example, recognize the problem of individualism (*gesellschaft*, anomie, and conflict), and Berger is equally cognizant of the problems of communalism (alienation). However, because they see them as essential problems, rooted in the structural conditions of the society in which they are found, they are presented as a fait accompli. Thus, anomie, conflict, and *gesellschaft* are understood as inevitable consequences of traditional society.[12] It is the dilemma, tragedy, and error of a fatalistic social science, confusing essential with derived problematics.

Biblical Possibilities. When these issues are seen from a biblical perspective, however, a whole new world of possibilities unfolds. First, if these are derived and not essential problems, then immediately the burden of inevitability is lifted. Anomie, for example, is not the unalterable consequence of modernity. It derives from the essential error, embodied in individualism, of denying our God-given need for human relationships. And while individualism is an error to which pluralistic societies are highly susceptible, it is certainly not structurally determined. Rather, it is the *easiest* form of denial in a pluralistic society, one we should be alert to but one that can be avoided.

It is worth repeating that a Christian approach to the social sciences is never fatalistic or deterministic. Whether the issue is anomie, alienation, conflict, or whatever, it will always be placed in the context of a derived problematic. As such, it may be viewed as a social manifestation of an essential problem, but not as the fundamental problem itself. One of the tasks of the Christian social scientist, it seems to me, is to discover the connections between essential and derived problematics, and from that basis to specify the types of denial, substitution, or combinations of the two most likely to occur in any given situation. Once such specification is accomplished, we should be in a position to understand and anticipate—not predict, in the fatalistic sense—empirical developments.

The second possibility opened up by a Christian approach—one implied in the first—is the opportunity for corrective action and change. To the fatalist, caught in the deterministic dilemma, the Christian social scientist must say, "Take heart—humanly initiated change is possible." To the functionalists and neo-Marxian conflict theorists, who try to avoid one problem by advocating another, the Christian social scientist must say, "No, a proper correction cannot be based on denial or substitution." Instead, genuine change will only occur as the result of a two-pronged effort aimed at dealing with both essential and derived problematics. In the face of the essential problem there must be proclamation of ultimate reconciliation through Jesus Christ. The derived problem implies that a Christian social-scientific perspective must always call us back to biblical relational norms as the basis for all social and cultural forms. Without them we will have little success avoiding the problems of denial and substitution.

Finally, a Christian perspective exposes us to a fuller understanding of sin. The good news that we are not locked into a fait accompli—that there can be genuine change—must not obscure the existence, power, or effects of sin. One of the responsibilities of a Christian social scientist, therefore, is to clearly expose the social, psychological, economic, and political devastation resulting from sin's influence.

Exposing the influence of sin, of course, will often be a thankless task, one certainly not appreciated by the world and sometimes not even by other Christians. Sin is not pretty, and people, Christians included, do not want to see it, either in their personal lives or in social conditions. Even fellow social scientists, usually adept at unearthing various problems, will not always be pleased with such discoveries. They, too, find it difficult to tolerate the notion of sin, and they are sometimes involved in the duplicity of the cover-up (e.g., the functional analysis of conflict). Nevertheless, Christian social scientists must always lay bare the reality of sin. This is part of the task of proclamation. It is essential, both to an understanding of truth and as a precursor of the always hoped-for possibility of reconciliation.

Chapter 12

DENIAL AND CREATION

Earlier we discussed God's intention for the relationship between humanity and the rest of creation. It was noted that the human being not only was to be a steward and caretaker of creation but also was to exercise dominion over it and to subdue it. We need to keep in mind, however, that, according to the biblical record, sin interfered with humanity's relationship to creation. In particular, sin made the task of caretaking and the responsibility of dominion much more difficult than it was originally intended to be. Because of the Fall, the earth yields its fruit stubbornly and creation provides its service with travail and much protestation.

Creation, therefore, presents itself to humanity in problematic form. In a sense, it is something like a sparring partner, one over which we exercise some degree of authority but which nevertheless continues to jab, parry, and frequently send us reeling to the mat. The question for humanity, therefore, is, How do we deal with creation? How do we approach this thing that always seems to be trying to prevent us from taking what we want and deserve? The answer to that question appears to center on the issue of sin. If we recognize that this sparring relationship results from humanity's sin, both past and present, then we must first deal with that problem before we can go about the task of setting up a creational relationship based on biblical norms and on the recognition that sin still abounds.

If, however, the issue of sin is ignored, then a whole different set of possibilities takes shape. For example, relationships may be expressed in one of the forms of substitution discussed earlier. Denial represents another possibility, and it is the one that specifically concerns us here. Returning to the sparring metaphor, denial occurs either when the sparring partner (creation) is allowed to beat incessantly upon humanity, or conversely, when humanity attempts to throw nothing but knock-out punches. The first option denies humanity's authority over creation while the second denies creation's intended place in relation to humanity. Because they appear to be easy methods of resolving humanity's relational dilemma with creation, both tendencies are likely when sin is ignored.

NATURISM

The denial of humanity's dominion over creation I will call "naturism." It is one possible expression of a naturalistic world view, and it may appear to be much like the type of substitution we called "creational humanism." There is one significant difference, however. Creational humanism elevates nature to the level of humanity and establishes the relationship on that basis. Thus, it encourages a kind of "brother earth" syndrome and denies that human beings have the right of dominion over creation. Naturism, on the other hand, disregards completely the issue of rights. It denies that human beings have the *ability* to exercise creational responsibilities and authority. Rather than a brother-earth syndrome, naturism is the carrier of creational fatalism, something of a "can't do" syndrome. It looks at the soaring mountain peaks and says, "We can't climb them"; it touches the rocky soil and says, "We can't farm it"; it feels the pain of disease and says, "We can't cure it." In short, it submits to the exigencies of the environment as if they were unalterable and beyond control.

Since work constitutes a rather visible means of relating to creation, it is an ideal repository for the values of naturism. The notion that work is something to be avoided or dreaded reflects this tendency, for it speaks to the power of creation over the individual. In Western society this takes the form of living for the weekend, working in order to retire, and suffering the proverbial Monday morning blues.[1] In history, the suggestion that the rich and powerful somehow ought to be free from the responsibilities of work also indicates these same values. Expressions of naturism suggest that while work is something that most people must do in order to survive, there is no satisfaction or duty in it. Rather, work represents the oppression of humanity by creation. If at all possible, it should be avoided.

If it weren't for the millions of Christians who appear to be caught up in weekend mania, we might be able to skip the obvious point that such a concept of work is patently nonbiblical. There is the half-truth that a sin-warped creation is not readily domesticated and many occupations are tedious, difficult, or worse. But the effect of sin on creation neither relieves us of our obligation to be caretakers nor denies us the possibility of enjoying stewardly tasks. When we make work (in the sense of "stewardship") our enemy, we give up one of our God-given privileges and we give in to the lie of naturism.

What this tells us, of course, is that naturism is seductive, in spite of its masochistic tendencies, precisely because it offers relief from creational responsibilities. If we admit that we have no power over nature, then we can relax in the luxury of irresponsibility and get on with the business of mere survival. Unfortunately, creation in its present condition is not an easy taskmaster, and it often makes even mere survival almost impossible. Naturism's deception is not in its warning that stewardship is difficult but in its suggestion that there is a viable passive alternative.

TECHNOLOGISM

Humanity's difficulties with creation can also be denied through "technologism." This happens whenever we seek to resolve our relational dilemma with creation not by addressing the issue of sin but by trying to exercise absolute control over the environment. In doing so, we deny our responsibility for the creation's marred condition as well as our obligation to preserve and maintain it for the Creator. We set ourselves up not as guardians but as exploiters and conquerors—potential victors in a contest with creation.

The reasons for this form of denial are not difficult to understand. Our relationship with nature is often frustrating. Nature presents us with calamities, disease, infertility, and sweat. Moreover, it is the carrier of death, and our lack of control over it only serves to remind us of our immortality. When this frustration is combined with our creational need to function as overseers, an equation exists that can easily result in exploitation and domination. It is an equation that is radically flawed because it fails to account for the source of the frustration.

The objective of technologism is the total subjugation of creation. It attempts to usurp God's position as proprietor and to set up humanity as lord of the environment. It is not satisfied with the role of guardian because that would eliminate the possibility of control. Nor is it satisfied with dominion, because that would require preservation. Technologism seeks to exercise unlimited power over creation, and it demands the right to use that power without regard to biblical norms or future generations.[2] Its overriding concern is to insulate humanity from any inconvenience that might be attributed to the environment.

Unlike naturism, technologism views work as an opportunity to gain influence over creation. Work is not perceived as inherently good, but it is valuable as a means of establishing control. Work under these circumstances can be enjoyable to the extent that it allows for the exercise of power, but it can also be evidence of personal failure if one is in an occupation with little authority or influence. For this reason, work represents something of a predicament for the inhabitants of the technological society. On the one hand, it has a high degree of social value because it is absolutely crucial to the goal of technologism. On the other hand, because its value is based on utility rather than stewardship, work is rarely personally rewarding or meaningful. This is a predicament with which those in the industrial West are quite familiar.

IMPLICATIONS

In the absence of biblical norms, therefore, one possibility is that human beings will rely upon naturism or technologism as the basis for their relationship with creation. Naturism will be more likely to occur in those societies where ultimate reality is based on a fatalistic perspective and, conversely, technologism will tend to exist in societies that embrace a humanistic concept of ultimate reality. However, because technologism and naturism can be embraced at both the personal and societal level, and since human beings apparently feel no need to be consistent on these matters, it is possible for these two approaches to coexist and intermingle.

As we have noted, the response of naturism is often "mere survival." This is particularly true when naturism is embedded in a society caught up in the denials of fatalism. When this occurs, there is a strong tendency toward the inhibition of human ingenuity in the realm of technology. As is the case with creational humanism, this inhibition can seriously retard the level of development. To put it simply, a society burdened by the values of naturism can easily miss opportunities for material and environmental improvement.

A crucial difference exists between creational humanism and naturism, however, a difference with developmental consequences. If exposed to the consequences of technological achievements, creational humanism will tend to be rigid and impenetrable, while naturism will be adaptive and flexible. In other words, the spirit of technology will find it far easier to make inroads in a society characterized by naturism than in a society in which creational humanism is dominant.[3] This is because creational humanism gives nature the right to exist without interference, while naturism is the passive expression of those who have given in to creational domination. Thus, when the wonders of technology are introduced, creational humanism views them as problems, while naturism views them as pyrrhic victories in a losing battle with nature. Moreover, because naturism conceives of work as something to be shunned, technological achievements are immediately attractive as potential mechanisms to avoid work.

Unfortunately, avoidance and unexpected victories do not provide much of a foundation for technological development. As a result, while technological innovations may be attractive to the patrons of naturism, rarely can they generate their own technological capacity. This point is especially important, it seems to me, in the modern context. For with rapid industrialization has come the coexistence of highly developed and underdeveloped societies and thus the easy exportation of technology and the possibilities of technology.

This means that underdeveloped societies with a naturistic orientation are extremely vulnerable both to outside environmental exploitation and to technological dependence. Environmental exploitation occurs because they have no values of stewardship or preservation with which to defend their ecological condition. Thus, they lack a reason to maintain their environment, particularly in the face of monetary pressure. Second, because they are receptive to technological innovation they can easily become dependent on outside sources to meet internal demand. Without the capability to generate indigenous technology, they are caught in the bind of being attached to technological products without the values to support their production.

Developed countries caught up in the wave of technologism, though free from naturism, are not free of the problematics of denial. For when men and women view themselves as agents of conquest, both they and creation turn out to be the losers. The problem here, of course, is lack of limits. If the goal is to beat creation into submission in order to use it to satisfy every human whim or craving, then there are virtually no restraints on those who have the power to accomplish such feats. Even arguments based upon self-interest, which plead for conservation and environmental protection for the sake of future generations, must fail when confronted by the force of technologism. The latter can always assert that future technology will enable future generations to handle future problems. Hope springs eternal from the wellspring of technologism.[4]

I will not take the time to elaborate on the myriad of social problems associated with technologism, in part because they have already been nauseatingly documented (in quadruplicate) elsewhere. Those with ears can readily hear the voices of despair; those with eyes—or any sense perception at all—can see the existence of these problems all around them. What interests us, and what is ultimately far more important, are the reasons that are given for these problems. Let us take a look at the predominant explanations.

First, we must recognize that the vast majority of individuals who live in a society permeated by technologism are committed to it. Thus, to the extent that they recognize the environmental problems associated with technological development, they do so purely within the context of "worlds yet to be conquered." Very simply then, they believe current problems will be resolved by future technological innovations. They point to history to support their case.

Second, there are those who look at problematic aspects of technological development and believe that it is evidence of the essentially problematic nature of technology. For them, technology is an evil whose benefits are illusory and whose general effect is to destroy the natural environment. They would suggest that humanity is better off repressing this hideous tendency and learning to live with, rather than battle against, its environment.

Third, there are those who locate themselves somewhere between these two extremes. They do not think that technology is inherently evil but they are not confident that our current problems will be resolved by future inventions. They tend to feel that, somewhere along the line, technology simply got out of hand. This occurred either because of the accelerated rate of technological development ("future shock") or because our values are not capable of changing rapidly enough to deal with technological change ("cultural lag").[5] As to whether modern industrial societies will be able to cope with these trends, this group renders a split decision. Some have faith that we can, while others are more dubious. Whatever the case, all of these represent "concerned citizens."

It would appear to me that all of these perspectives err because they fail to accurately access the nature of the problem. The first group is probably correct in assuming that there will be future technological breakthroughs. They are quite wrong, however, in asserting that these breakthroughs will solve our present predicament. History, while certainly showing a pattern of technological development and problem solving, also demonstrates a pattern of problem generation. It provides little assurance of problem resolution.

The second group is correct in proclaiming the imperative of living with the environment, but they are incorrect in assuming that technology necessarily interferes with that objective. For example, it would be hard to argue that those women of antiquity who died during childbirth because of lack of medical technology were somehow more successful at "living with their environment" than their modern counterparts. Technology is neither antithetical to human ecology nor inherently evil.

The third group is appropriately concerned about modern technological developments, but they err when they suggest that the source of concern is either the rapidity of technological development or the lumbering pace of correlative values. The problem is not pace; it is direction.

It is extremely important to understand, therefore, that the problem is not technology, but technologism. The issue at hand is not humanity's inability to change values fast enough but its propensity to use the wrong values. The future development, or termination, of humanity depends not so much on the kind of technology produced—though that is important—as on the values behind its production. When the objective is environmental conquest, human convenience, or natural isolation, then technology is doomed to self-destruction. Its appetite is limitless and constraints are nonexistent. Moreover, unless technological development is rooted in the value of stewardship, those who recognize its problematic effects are destined to dismiss them, to rebound to naturism, or to become stuck in the quagmire of an unresolvable dilemma. Since quagmires are not particularly satisfying, excesses of technologism will generally lead to a backlash of naturism.

CONCLUSION: TWO OBSERVATIONS

It would be unfortunate if the above discussion left the reader with the impression that a Christian perspective within the social sciences is capable only of specifying values. That is certainly not the case. I am suggesting, however, that to understand the relationship of human beings to their environment we will need to discover germane and operative values. Only then will we be in a position to explore and anticipate the political, economic, psychological, and sociological implications of any particular setting. This approach, I admit, will sound strange to those reared on traditional social science, since it runs counter to the assumption that values are derived purely from material conditions. But if the analysis of the human condition presented in this book is correct, this will be a far more insightful and productive point of departure than that of traditional social science.

One final comment. The problems associated with technologism, many of which have been experienced by the population of Western societies, have led some, including Christians, to postulate a kind of technological determinism. This position assumes that technological developments determine other forms of social development. Some who hold to this assumption attempt to be consistent, applying it to all societies at all times. Most, however, believe that it is especially applicable in the context of the modern industrial society. The latter feel that with industrialization has come a new form of technology, one beyond human management and literally out of control. It is something like the robot that has turned on its master.

From the perspective of the relational dilemma, however, technological determinism is really a latent form of naturism. It implies that humanity's relationship with the environment is beyond human control and that all attempts to exercise dominion will eventually fail or backfire. Thus, those technological determinists who decry the modern state of affairs—and most do—almost always assume that there is at least a kernel of evil at the heart of technology.

It is important to remember, therefore, that while technological determinists make some valid points about technological problematics as well as some cogent implied criticisms of technologism, they are essentially expressing an antithetical form of denial. Their only solution to the problem of technology is a "less-is-better" philosophy and a retreat from humanity's creational responsibilities. But while at times less may indeed be better, this is by no means a foregone conclusion or an appropriate philosophical guideline. A Christian approach to the social sciences would be well advised not to fall in step with the rhetoric of technological determinism.

Chapter 13

CONCLUSION: PRESENT PREDICAMENTS AND FUTURE BUILDING PROJECTS

We have come a great distance. Between the first argument about the nature of assumptions and the last discussion of the effects of technologism, there have been numerous points, subpoints, and not a few sidetracks. But beyond the details and academic excursions, two overriding objectives have remained constant.

The first was to gain some understanding of the nature of assumptions and how divergent assumptions influence our thinking and doing. My primary concern, of course, was to examine the effect of assumptions on "scientific" thinking and doing and to contrast the impact of Christian assumptions with those typically employed in the sciences today. My conclusion was that the social sciences, in contemporary form, are not only dependent upon naturalistic assumptions, but also are suffering the consequences of such dependency. For the Christian, I suggested, there ought to be an alternative.

Part B, therefore, pursued a second objective: to consider social science subject matter from the perspective of Christian assumptions. Working from a biblically informed philosophy of science, we attempted (1) to gain a biblical appreciation of the human condition, and (2) to discover its ramifications for the study of human relationships. The relational dilemma provided the framework for this investigation. Its application enabled us to explore the implications of two illegitimate relational forms—substitution and denial. This framework, however, was not designed to provide a definitive methodology for Christian social scientists, but to serve as a vehicle for Christian thinking about the study and content of the social sciences. If it has accomplished that purpose, even in part, it has fulfilled my intent.

ON PRESENT PREDICAMENTS . . .

I wish to conclude, however, not with a summary of objectives, but with two brief comments. At the time of this writing, my youngest daughter is just over a year old. One parental obligation, for which I sometimes admit responsibility, is her breakfast feeding. Despite my familiarity with this task, I am forever amazed at what transpires during these occasions. In particular, I remain dumbfounded by her ability to ingest great quantities of oatmeal. Even though she only weighs about twenty pounds, she will consume an adult portion of oatmeal at a pace only constrained by the speed at which I am able to move the spoon from the oatmeal to her mouth. Her appetite at breakfast is nearly insatiable. Indeed, at the end of the meal, though I am exhausted, she still wants more.

As we come to the close of this treatise, I suspect that many readers may feel as if they had just experienced one of my daughter's breakfasts. For some, like my daughter, the meal went too quickly—too many questions were left unanswered: too many issues left unaddressed. For these, the book merely skimmmed the surface of an extremely important topic. Other readers, however, may identify more readily with the fate of the father, feeling as if they have been dragged through an amazing event at breath-taking speed. They would have preferred a more leisurely pace, along with a smaller bowl of porridge.

With both groups, I have much sympathy. Indeed, my greatest challenge has been to bridge these two communities and attempt to address both the world of the expert (for whom every question merits a detailed answer) and that of the interested novice (for whom every question leads into unchartered—and potentially murky—waters). In all honesty, I have not always felt adequately equipped for this challenge. And yet, regardless of whether the reader feels exhausted or merely teased by the contents of this book, for the experience itself, I do not apologize. The issue at stake is far too important to be left only to the experts and far too complex to be adequately addressed by the novice alone.

. . . AND FUTURE BUILDING PROJECTS

The "issue," of course, is nothing less than the future of the social sciences. That sounds a bit melodramatic, I know, but it appears to be accurate. The question facing every social scientist is this: What shall be the guiding assumptions of my work? And yet that is a question rarely asked by modern students of the human condition. Some fail to ask it because they have simply appropriated, without comment, the assumptions of their masters; they have dutifully imbibed the thoughts of the status quo. Others, a bit bolder perhaps, may have probed the issue (possibly in a theory course—or more likely, a course in the philosophy of science). But upon doing so, they have been told that they are swimming in sacred waters. The guiding assumptions of the discipline are set by the requirements of objective science, they have been told, and such requirements are not to be contravened.

Questions rarely asked are usually important. Certainly that is the case here, for the theory, research, and analyses of social problems during the coming years hangs on the question of assumptions. What is true and what are the implications of that truth for the social sciences? This is such a simple question and yet one almost universally ignored in the social sciences today. It is ignored because few moderns, scientist or otherwise, can supply an answer. And so, instead of asking the question, the modern social scientist "looks for truth" in the context of the preexistent assumptions of his discipline. Since these latent assumptions are exclusively naturalistic, when truths are discovered in the social sciences today, they seem (remarkably!) to support a naturalistic world view.

It should tell us something when disciplines whose fundamental objective is the discovery of truth ignore the question at
the onset of their inquiry. Something about our age. Something
about the products of our age, of which the social sciences are
only one. And something about the responsibilities, in such an
age, of those who call themselves Christians.

From the house of social science today, both the Master
Builder and the Cornerstone have been banished, and those
who labor in construction do so without much knowledge of its
foundation. If that were not distressing enough, many modern
Christians seem resolved to either joining the construction
project as is or damning the structure from Mount Sinai. In
duplicity or damnation, let us have no part. Let us, rather,
build a house where gods may dwell, and where the only
God—the Creator—is Lord.

LAMENTATIONS AND APPROBATIONS

According to Webster, an epilogue is "a closing section added to a novel, play, etc., providing further comment, interpretation, or information." That being the case, one might describe the following as an appendage to an "etc."! However, to be more precise (and a bit more helpful), I would like to examine here some of the "yeas" and "nays" of a Christian approach to the social sciences—both those attributes that should be cultivated as well as those that should be shunned. The list is not exhaustive, but it does represent many of the issues that will confront Christians intent on approaching the social sciences in a holistic fashion.

Needless to say, there is a good deal of subjectivity in an effort of this kind. Indeed, the contents of this chapter grew out of my own experience with the issue of Christian scholarship (otherwise known as the "integration of faith and learning"). Some of these were personal experiences, with Christians and non-Christians alike, who were either jubilant or incredulous about the idea of a Christian social science perspective. Others were purely cognitive encounters, resulting from my readings on a number of topics. Whatever their source, such experiences have convinced me that there are a series of recurring themes, both in the critiques of and attempts at Christian scholarship.

Some of these themes seem helpful while others appear highly problematic. What follows is an attempt to sort through a few of them in a manner that will be useful both to the jubilant as well as to the incredulous.

A CHRISTIAN APPROACH TO THE
SOCIAL SCIENCES IS NOT . . .

Dogmatic. One of the first accusations likely to be leveled at a Christian attempt in the social sciences is that it is too dogmatic to be a part of the scientific enterprise. Given the discussion in part A of this book, one might suspect that such an accusation contains a good deal of naivete, both about the history of dogmatism in science and about the meaning of a "Christian" science. Setting aside that broader philosophical dispute, however, I would simply like to say that a Christian social scientific perspective ought to be less—not more—dogmatic than its contemporary counterpart. I say this for three reasons.

First, the Christian social scientist will tend not to absolutize his discoveries. Anyone familiar with human science literature knows that it is common for theorists to take a set of observations and build not only a theory upon them but also a definition of reality (e.g., Skinner, Marx, and Freud). They do this often without understanding the assumptions that enabled them to make their observations. Christian social scientists, however, will view such observations as derived rather than essential truths. Their observations will be seen as *relative* to their assumptive framework and *fragmentary* with respect to the whole of reality. Thus, the Christian social scientist does not absolutize findings but seeks to understand them in the context of the larger whole. While it is true that Christian social scientists believe there are essential truths (which must themselves be interpreted), that fact does not incline them toward dogmatism. Indeed, it is precisely because they have an appreciation for essential truth that they can distinguish it from the fragments and thereby refrain from being dogmatic about the latter.

Second, a Christian social science does not require nonparticipating social scientists to operate on the basis of its assumptions. Nor does it deny the legitimacy of social science efforts constructed within other frameworks, though it certainly may deny their claims to truth. It assumes that science will best be served by a genuine pluralism that allows all scientists to build freely upon their chosen assumptions. Unlike objective science, which argues that every scientist must conform to its assumptions to assure impartiality, a Christian social science assumes that scientific integrity will be best served by philosophical candor and a clear explanation of assumptions.

Finally, Christian efforts in the social sciences should function within the constraints of scientific humility. Because their world view assumes that human beings are finite, limited, and prone to sin, Christian social scientists should be characterized by caution and humility in their judgments. Christians, regardless of their professions, who operate in a closed world of dogmatism and snap judgments are simply not being true to their own convictions. Many Marxists and not a few humanists, I might add, would find their own presuppositions much less limiting.

Imperialistic. Because a Christian approach to the social sciences is not dogmatic, it is for similar reasons not imperialistic. It does not attempt to dominate the explanation of any particular phenomenon but rather recognizes the validity of a variety of disciplinary perspectives. Once again, it views scientific discoveries in the light of the whole, not trying to define reality on the basis of particularistic observations but always seeking to integrate them into the larger picture.

In my opinion, this tendency should differentiate a Christian effort in the social sciences from much of contemporary social science. So many modern scholars seem driven to reinterpret the world on the basis of their own novel observations, no matter how narrow or limited they may be. At times, they resemble arrogant, opinionated children bent on ignoring the insights and legitimacy of other perspectives. Christian social scientists should never be so inclined. Neither the humility implied in their assumptions nor their respect for the object of their analyses (humanity) allows such behavior.

Pessimistic-Optimistic. Though some may worry about what

they perceive as the dogmatic tendencies in a Christian social science, my fear is that it will be seduced by the temptations of pessimism and optimism. I base this concern on personal experience. It is so easy, for example, to focus exclusively on social problems as a Christian because they represent evidence of sin, a phenomenon that Christians certainly must take seriously. However, while Christian social scientists must always expose the empirical manifestations of sin, they must never do so by denying either God's good creation, the possibility that human beings can make genuinely good choices, or the potential for problem solving.

Conversely, it is also easy to experience the goodness of God's creation and to emphasize this at the expense of sin. Of course, God's creation *is* good, and He gives us much to be thankful for. But while a Christian social scientist will want to affirm God's creativity as well as human possibilities, he or she cannot do so without at the same time pointing out the reality and terrible consequences of sin. The relational problem is real. Our only source of ultimate confidence is in the solution God has provided.

Both pessimism and optimism result from a fixation on one aspect of the relational dilemma. Christian social scientists, of all people, should be sensitive to the fallacy of such a fixation and should be careful not to let it creep into their scientific discourses.

Dialectic. For many, both inside and outside Christendom, reality presents itself in antithetical form, as an inescapable conflict between two opposing forces. Sometimes this conflict is seen to be marginally productive, but usually it is viewed as patently pathological (a few authors think it is both at the same time). Marx's dialectic based upon class conflict is probably the most well known, but dialectic is also present in the approaches of such varied thinkers as Freud, Barth, and Ellul. Sociologists often conceive of the *gemeinschaft-gesellschaft* typology in dialectical terms while theologians sometimes understand "good and evil" or the "God-human" relationship as dialectical phenomena. All hold in common the assumption that conflict is a necessary imperative of human existence.

While I am personally indebted to the thoughts of many

who consider themselves dialectical thinkers, I must demur from embracing their assumptions. From a biblical perspective, though such thinkers may accurately perceive the relational dilemma, they fail to fully appreciate the possibility of its resolution. As a result, they are enamored with the conflict produced by the groaning of God's creation under the burden of sin and myopic about other eventualities. This tends not only to cultivate fatalism, but a real void of prescriptive alternatives. Many dialectical thinkers, for example, have a great deal of difficulty presenting viable solutions of any kind. They are quite content to let us know by which horn of the dilemma we are presently being skewered. Those with solutions, moreover, hold up utopian futures, such as classlessness or pie-in-the-sky theology, that bear little resemblance to reality or life. Whatever the case, I believe they are in serious error.

We cannot deny that conflict abounds all around us and that it is likely to do so until God's final solution. Nevertheless, conflict is not an imperative of any particular relationship at any particular point in time. Relationships *can* be based on biblical norms. As Christ reconciles us to God, so can He reconcile us to one another. Relationships can be redeemed, restored, and set right. Yes, they will not stay that way forever. Yes, many will not experience any degree of redemption at all. But, and this is an important "but," we cannot deny the possibility of redemption. To do so is not only to eliminate God-given hope but to infringe upon one of His prerogatives. We simply have no business limiting God's options through human dialectics.

Dualistic. Finally, we should mention something that can only be described as a ploy. Yet this ploy seems to have been successfully foisted on many within the Christian scientific community today. It is dualistic thinking—the idea that the world of God and the world of scientific explanation are mutually exclusive. This dualism assumes that God causes everything *except* what we can explain in nonmiraculous terms. Whether the subject is lightning, conception, or the parting of the Red Sea, the assumption seems to be that if science can explain it, God could not have caused it. As a result, over the last few hundred years as science has enlarged the realm of its explanatory orbit, God's realm has decreased proportionately.

Ironically, this way of thinking judges God's influence negatively to the degree that He made creation orderly and understandable.

Though this tendency is evident among Christians in both the physical and social sciences, it may be more problematic for those whose disciplines take them into the heart of human affairs. It is one thing to have lightning described as an orderly sequence of events; it is quite another to have one's mate selection, conversion experience, or favorite passage of Scripture so described. Whether or not such an interpretation *should* disturb us, however, depends not on the assumption of order but on the framework of assumptions in which the interpretation is found. A Christian ought to be troubled, for example, by a purely naturalistic interpretation of human (or physical) events. But the assumption that human beings do things in an orderly fashion, using similar motives and rationale, should not by itself cause such disquiet. Nor should we assume, for that matter, that God does not use common experiences to effect His will. Indeed, given the kind of orderly universe He has created, we ought to be somewhat surprised, though not perplexed, when He chooses to operate otherwise. Whatever the case, we must not limit God to the world of the miraculous. A god so limited is a puny replica of the real thing.

When Christian social scientists fall prey to dualistic thinking, they seem to do one of two things. First, some become Christian iconoclasts, prophesying against all evidence of scientifically predictable tendencies within the Christian community. Their assumption is that if something is truly God-inspired it cannot be scientifically explained. Thus, the world of "genuine Christianity" shrinks with every scientific observation, and the Christian iconoclast is confined to a faith of the mysterious, ineffable, and personal. The second possibility is that the dualist will simply discard the faith. To the extent that God is confined to the unexplainable, the dualist soon discovers that success as a social scientist is inversely related to the size of his or her god. Not surprisingly, the best "Christian" social scientists operating under this assumption are the least likely to keep the faith.

Whatever the consequences, let me be clear about what

dualism seeks to accomplish. First, it arbitrarily sets the parameters for God's influence, often employing the secular-sacred distinction. Second, it judges God's worldly involvement on that basis. But God has given us only one criterion for discerning His involvement: "goodness." God is the source of all that is "good," whether found in creation, relationships, or Christian communities. Additional criteria are not only uncalled for, they are pregnant with tragic implications. As Christian social scientists, we would be well advised to jettison false criteria rather than our faith.

A CHRISTIAN APPROACH TO THE SOCIAL SCIENCES IS . . .

Value-laden. If anything was communicated in the first few chapters of this book, I trust it was this: where values are concerned, there is no such thing as a vacuum. Every decision, every observation, every act, every *everything*, occurs in the confines of values. The fact that two or more people agree on a particular observation, or anything, does not mean that their observation or the thing they are observing stands alone as some autonomous reality. It merely indicates that they share, at some point, a common interpretative framework. What we perceive with our senses is always related to what we believe about the world, our senses, etc., and everything that exists is related in some fashion to its Creator.

A few points of clarification may help. First, the fact that everything is woven in a fabric of values does not imply that everything *is* a value. Certainly, values need to be distinguished from other types of phenomena. What I find unacceptable is the assumption that some things exist outside of a value framework. It is the issue of autonomy, not differentiation, that concerns me.

Second, my position on values should not suggest that a Christian effort within the social sciences is a deductive rather than an inductive enterprise. The task of the Christian social scientist does not revolve exclusively around the deduction of theoretical insights from the perspective of Christian values. Although this is an important activity and the area where I have concentrated my efforts, the Christian social scientist should be just as concerned about the integration of specific observations within their value framework. It is the value "relatedness" of knowledge, not its deduction, that the Christian social scientist finds imperative.

Third, it is my opinion that the value relatedness of the scientific task should make Christians hesitant about using certain kinds of language in scholarly discourse. When we say that something (e.g., a finding) is "neutral," or "neither good nor bad," or an "is" as opposed to an "ought," we often obscure or deny its valuative implications. Common usage would suggest, for example, that "is" represents a neutral point of agreement wholly unrelated to the issue of values. But such an assumption is not congruent with the biblical picture of God's creation.

Finally, it should be pointed out that while knowledge exists within a value framework, all statements do not imply a value "judgment." This does not mean that they are therefore value-free statements. It simply suggests that their location has not yet been defined (i.e., they are "meaning-less"). When someone says that "33 percent of the automobiles in Romania are white" and nothing else, thus isolating the statement from any meaningful context, we will want to admit that its value implications are indeterminable. But we ought not to agree that it is therefore a neutral fact. To do so would disengage the thing from God. We are in no position to do that.

Assumptive. Because Christian social scientists recognize the role of values within their discipline, they should be as explicit as possible about the assumptive content of their approaches. Authors should not play cat and mouse games with their readers, disguising presuppositions in the vain hope of producing a value-free social science. That leads neither to clarity of thought nor to genuine communication. Instead, a detailed explanation of assumptions and a willingness to be as candid as possible about presuppositional issues should characterize a Christian approach to the social science. Such an approach, I believe, will serve the scientific community far better than current efforts at objectivity.

Prophetic. A consciously Christian social science will also be consciously prophetic. Just as it does not attempt to cloak its value assumptions, it is similarly frank about the implications of those assumptions for the world of social science. In so doing, it differs only in candidness from objective science. *All* meaningful discussions in the social sciences have prophetic implications. Despite a century of arguments to the contrary, in moments of personal candor, most social scientists know this to be true. It is a pity we cannot all admit it and get on with the essential tasks in social science.

Quite possibly, one of the reasons we have such difficulty admitting this fact is that we live with a grotesque picture of the social science prophet. We imagine such folk to be paranoid, alienated types, projecting their frustrations on the world around them without regard for logic, careful study, or thorough analysis. While such a caricature may aptly describe some who have chosen to vent their values, it should not describe the Christian social scientist.

Let me be clear about what I mean by a consciously prophetic social science. First, I do not mean dogmatism, closed-mindedness, or lack of rigor. Those options simply are not available to anyone attempting a systematic understanding of the human condition within the context of a Christian world view. Everything I have said in this manuscript about Christian social scientific thinking mitigates against such a posture. What I do mean to suggest, however, is that a "Christian" social science (1) will be explicit about its assumptions, (2) will specify relevant biblical values, (3) will make value judgments (whenever the scientist's understanding of the situation permits such judgments), and (4) will point human beings back to their biblical moorings. Nothing about this approach implies pigheadedness or prophetic conceit. Indeed, we ought to be deeply suspicious of prophetic pronouncements by social scientists that serve the prophet more than they do the discipline.

Integrative. All knowledge finds its coherence in the Creator. That includes knowledge about human relationships or any other topic within the social sciences. A fundamental assumption of the Christian social scientist, therefore, is that empirical insights exist within a coherent and interrelated framework. Certainly finite human beings will not be able, even if willing, to *fully* understand such interrelationships. But ultimately, they do exist. For that reason, as much as humanly possible, a Christian approach to the social sciences ought to be characterized by integrative efforts and a concern for comprehensive understanding.

Contemporary social science is not characterized by integration but a high degree of specificity. This presents both an opportunity and a great danger. The opportunity takes the form of increased possibilities for in-depth understanding of the human condition. The danger, however, is that specialization may not lead to understanding at all, but simply a shopping list of disparate and unrelated observations or theories. Our concern here is not simply with abstracted empiricism. Though that continues to be a problem, it is one with which most social scientists are familiar. The larger problem is what might be termed "abstracted theory"—the tendency to neither relate theories to one another (within a discipline or across disciplines) nor integrate them into a broader understanding of the human condition. This leads, I believe, to a real myopia about the breadth and complexity of human relationships. With such narrow vision, is it any wonder that limited theories writ large (e.g., Marxism) gain such a popular following?

It would be wrong to conclude that the Christian social scientist is unconcerned about the finer details of human existence or that he or she is somehow predisposed against "hard" data. (The notion of hard data, by the way, is an artifact of objective science; it incorrectly differentiates between what it considers real [hard] and interpreted [soft] data.) Specificity ought to be an important component of a Christian social scientific effort, to the benefit, not at the expense, of a deeper understanding of the human condition. We must reject abstracted knowledge, not details.

Appreciative. In the final analysis, Christian social scientists ought to be appreciative, both of the scientific task and of the creature God has allowed them to study. Frankly, I worry about those social scientists who seem so weighed down by the burden of inquiry that their only pleasure comes in debunking and their only joy in pulling others into the morass of their own pathological analyses. Such may be the dilemma of a social science in search of its moorings but not one rooted in Christian assumptions.

Eric Liddle, the gold medal Olympian from Scotland portrayed in the film "Chariots of Fire," is reported to have said, "When I run, I feel God's pleasure." He did not mean, certainly, that every aspect of the task was enjoyable. There is great pain and difficult work involved in becoming an accomplished runner. But the determination to use what God had given him, and to use it well, allowed him the opportunity to "feel God's pleasure." I can think of no greater joy, nor higher calling.

I trust that Christian social scientists will be able to feel that same pleasure. We have no reason not to. Stretched before us is the wonder of God's creation, massively scarred but marvelously redeemable. Planted deeply within us is the reflection of God's own image, sprouting with shoots of curiosity, discovery, and understanding. And between the two lies nothing but vast possibilities, for good as well as ill. It is for goodness sake that we must chart our course. It is for God's pleasure that we must follow it.

NOTES

NOTES

Part A

[1] See Alvin A. Gouldner, *The Coming Crisis of Western Sociology* (New York: Avon, 1970), for a perceptive though somewhat hackneyed critique of the state of contemporary sociological thought.

Chapter 1

[1] Often the scientist working within a particular paradigm does not perceive this. He or she tends to think of the history of science as a methodical, evolutionary movement whose progress is determined by the discovery of facts. Such a view of scientific history, though supported by the modern scientific textbook seems to be contradicted by the evidence. As Kuhn, Feyerabend, and others have shown, there is a great deal of interpretive conflict and controversy in the history of modern science.

[2] Much of our discussion about Durkheim comes from his classic study of religion, *Elementary Forms of the Religious Life,* trans. Joseph W. Swain (1915; reprint, New York: Free Press, 1965). Interested readers should also see *The Rules of Sociological Method* (1893; reprint, New York: Free Press, 1958); *The Division of Labor in Society,* trans. G. Simpson (1893; reprint, New York: Free Press, 1960); and *Suicide: A Study in Sociology,* trans. Spaulding and Simpson (1897; reprint, New York: Free Press, 1951).

[3] Durkheim, *Elementary Forms of the Religious Life,* 347. An interesting extension of Durkheim's argument is found in Guy Swanson's, *The Birth of the Gods* (Ann Arbor: University of Michigan Press, 1968).

[4] This problem exists not only at the metaphysical level but also at the point of theory construction and methodological application. For a discussion of this problem in the "Protestant Ethic" debate, see S. D. Gaede, "Religious Affiliation, Social Mobility, and the Problem of Causality: A Methodological Critique of Protestant-Catholic Socioeconomic Achievement Studies," *Review of Religious Research,* vol. 19, no. 1 (Fall 1977): 54–62.

[5] This reflects my own view that much research in the social and behavioral sciences has aped methods of the physical (or so-called natural) sciences without much evidence of success. Please see Alasdair MacIntyre, *After Virtue* (Notre Dame: University of Notre Dame Press, 1981).

Chapter 2

[1]Gerhard Lenski, *Human Societies* (New York: McGraw-Hill, 1970), 502, has defined world views as "men's beliefs about the ultimate nature of reality; their interpretation of the totality of experience." I have drawn from his discussion of this concept for my understanding and interpretation.

[2]One of the contributions of differential association theory, it seems to me, is the insight that even much so-called deviant behavior is not an expression of idiosyncrasy but collective behavior. The earliest statement of this is found in Edwin Sutherland, *Criminology* (New York: Lippincott, 1924).

[3]Certainly this could be debated. My purpose at this point, however, is not to present a definitive argument concerning which world views have been most influential in Western society, but to demonstrate how a particular world view affects one's thinking about science.

[4]I am defining naturalism a little more broadly than is commonly the case in the field of philosophy. Arthur Danto provides an adequate survey of naturalism in the *Encyclopedia of Philosophy*, ed. Edwards (New York: Macmillan and Free Press, 1967), 5:448. Danto recommends "Naturalism and First Principles" and "Nature and the Human Spirit," in Sidney Hook's *The Quest for Being* (New York: Dell, 1961) for a sympathetic treatment of naturalism.

[5]This is an obviously pejorative statement, made from the perspective of a theist. Some naturalists might want to argue that the universe is not necessarily "ordered" (though then they might have difficulty explaining their confidence in science), and certainly they would all assert that chance is not "blind." Blindness assumes the existence of a Being who cannot see; the naturalist, strictly speaking, assumes no Being at all. From my perspective as a Christian, however, this is a wholly accurate statement. The world certainly is ordered, and the naturalist's explanation of it as a chance occurrence seems to assume that this order, as well as our understanding of it, came without foresight or direction—that is, blind chance.

[6]Some are more blatant than others, however. One of the better recently published texts in sociology, for example, begins with Hu Shih's statement: "Only when we realize that there is no eternal, unchanging truth or absolute truth can we arouse in ourselves a sense of responsibility. The knowledge that mankind needs is not the way or principle which has an absolute existence, but the particular truths for here and now." See Kenneth Westhues, *First Sociology* (New York: McGraw-Hill, 1982).

[7]For a good discussion of a variety of issues related to determinism, see Sydney Hook, ed. *Determinism and Freedom in the Age of Modern Science* (Washington Square, N.Y.: New York University Press, 1958).

⁸This is not the concept of materialism used in everyday parlance, which relates to the human desire for material goods. Rather, we are here discussing materialism as it often occurs in the social sciences—an explanation of events which relies exclusively upon material determinants. When Karl Marx explained social and political revolutions (and the human actions that precipitated them) purely in terms of class conditions, he was being a consistent materialist.

⁹In William L. Reese, *Dictionary of Philosophy and Religion: Eastern and Western Thought* (Atlantic Highlands, N.J.: Humanities Press, 1980), 409–10, "pantheism" is defined as follows: "From the Greek 'pan' and 'theos' meaning 'everything is God'. The adjective 'pantheist' was introduced by John Toland in 1705 in reference to Socinianism. In an attack on Toland in 1709, Fay characterized Toland's position as 'pantheism'. Once introduced, the term was applied to a variety of positions where God and the world are held to be identical." Reese distinguishes between a number of types of pantheism, stemming from both Eastern and Western thought.

¹⁰An example of this trend in the physical sciences is Fritjof Capra's, *The Tao of Physics: An Exploration of the Parallels Between Modern Physics and Eastern Mysticism* (Berkeley: Shambhala, 1975).

¹¹A comparative understanding of major world views and their assumptions can be found in Huston Smith's lucid, if slippery, book, *The Religions of Man* (New York: Harper and Row, 1965).

Chapter 3

¹A good discussion of the development of modern science can be found in R. Hooykaas, *Religion and the Rise of Modern Science* (Grand Rapids: Eerdmans, 1972); for a standard interpretation, see A. Rupert Hall, *The Revolution in Science: 1500–1750* (New York: Longman, 1983).

²Alfred North Whitehead's argument is one of the best known; see his *Science and the Modern World* (New York: Macmillan, 1948); see also Robert K. Merton, "Puritanism, Pietism and Science," *Social Theory and Social Structure* (New York: Free Press, 1964), 574–606.

³See Alan Storkey, *A Christian Social Perspective* (Leicester, U.K.: InterVarsity, 1979), 80.

⁴See Merton, "Puritanism, Pietism and Science," 574–606.

⁵Storkey, *A Christian Science Perspective*, 80.

⁶One gets a flavor of this by reading biographies of some of the earlier European scientists; see, for example, Richard Westfall, *Never at Rest: A Biography of Isaac Newton* (Cambridge: Cambridge University Press, 1980); and Arthur Koestler, *The Watershed: A Biography of Johannes Kepler* (Garden City, N.Y.: Doubleday, 1960).

[7]The Creation accounts in Genesis 1 and 2 make this point abundantly clear: "And God saw everything that he had made, and behold, it was very good. And there was evening and there was morning, a sixth day" (Gen. 1:31 RSV).

[8]See Genesis 1:28; 2:15.

[9]This statement does not imply an acceptance, on my part, of naive realism in perception. Though that may have been the assumption of these early scientists, it seems untenable to me. I would agree with Bert Hodges ("Perception Is Relative and Veridical," unpublished manuscript, Gordon College, 1983) that perception can be *both* relative and truthful.

Chapter 4

[1]It is always a mystery to me that theologians, who claim to hold Christian assumptions, can speak for God on so many topics about which the Lord Himself remains quiet. True, they build their interpretations upon God's Word—at least I would hope so. But these are the interpretations of finite beings. Such a realization ought to inspire humility, not arrogance.

[2]I do not want to give the impression here that Christians were uninvolved in the production and dissemination of Enlightenment thought. Clearly, some were. John Locke, for example, in *The Reasonableness of Christianity* (1695), argued that since God (who made man in His own image) is the author of reason, the truths of the Christian faith could be demonstrated by rational thought. In so doing, he made reason the evaluator of God, and enabled Christians to join the Enlightenment's praise of rational man. God, of course, *is* the author of reason; but He is not reasonable, or tame, or capable of being fully understood by His creation.

[3]For a general discussion of Enlightenment thought and its development, see Harold G. Nicolson, *The Age of Reason* (London: Constable, 1960); also Peter Gay, *The Enlightenment, An Introduction* (New York: Knopf, 1966). For a discussion of the relationship of Enlightenment thought and the social sciences, see Storkey, *A Christian Social Perspective*, 24–35.

[4]"Objective science" is a somewhat ambiguous term since it means different things to different people. As will be clear, our use of the term has nothing to do with the need to be fair, ethical, or truthful in scientific discussion. Rather, by "objective science" we are referring to the possibility of being value-neutral or assumption-free as a scientist. Ethical behavior is a requirement of good science; "objective science" is an impossibility. Those desiring to read arguments against our position should see Karl Popper, *Objective Knowledge: An Evolution-*

ary Approach (London: Oxford University Press, 1972); the best such argument in the social sciences is found in Peter Berger and Hansfried Kellner, *Sociology Reinterpreted: An Essay on Method and Vocation* (Garden City, N.Y.: Doubleday, 1981); their argument is profoundly present-ed—and, I believe, profoundly wrong as well.

Chapter 5

[1] David Hume's (1711–1776) objective, particularly in *A Treatise of Human Nature* (New York: Oxford University Press, 1951), and *Enquiry Concerning Human Understanding* (New York: Oxford University Press, 1951), was a little different than mine, of course, since he was interested in why humans think that every event must have a cause. In the course of answering that question, however, he argued (convinc-ingly, I think) that the relationship between an event and its putative cause is neither intuitively obvious nor demonstrable. That is precisely what I have called the "problem of certainty" in science.

[2] See Karl Popper, *The Logic of Scientific Discovery* (New York: Basic Books, 1959).

[3] Nicholas Wolterstorff, *Reason Within the Bounds of Religion* (Grand Rapids: Eerdmans, 1976), 38.

[4] This was the date of the first edition of Thomas Kuhn's *The Structure of Scientific Revolutions* (Chicago: University of Chicago Press, 1962). Several important revisions have occurred since that time.

[5] Please see Margaret Masterman, "The Nature of a Paradigm," *Criticism and the Growth of Knowledge,* ed. Imre Lakatos and Alan Musgrave (Cambridge: Cambridge University Press, 1970).

[6] Drawing on the work of Gibson, Hodges in "Perception as Relative and Veridical" (unpublished manuscript, Gordon College, 1983) argues, successfully I think, that perception is a relative busi-ness, and yet we have grounds for believing the relative truth which our eyes see. Relativism is another slippery term, however, since it may mean something quite different in one area (e.g., perception) than it does in another (e.g., values, ethics, etc.). My point is simply that Christians should not overreact to problems in ethical relativism by jettisoning the idea altogether or by assuming that relative claims are necessarily wrong.

[7] I know that I will be roundly condemned for making this assertion, since many naturalistic scientists do, in fact, work within a highly developed ethical system. I hope such condemnation is justified and that my conclusion is wrong. However, nothing I have seen so far is much of a balm.

Most ethical systems advocated by naturalists either assert the value of humanity in an a priori fashion (in which case it is more accurate to call them humanists than naturalists—humanists do, indeed, have a well articulated ethical agenda), or they explain the need for ethics as a necessity for survival (in which case it becomes an essentially selfish act, and thus unnecessary if not in the self-interest). I fail to see how the assumptions of naturalism, however, lead to a compelling ethic, able to convince the holder that obedience to the ethic is more important than self-interest.

Chapter 6

[1] I am using the terms "social science" and "human sciences" interchangeably (knowing that both designations are offensive to some readers) to refer to those disciplines which attempt the scientific study of aspects of humanity. In that, we are including anthropology, economics, political science, psychology, and sociology; history might also be included, depending upon one's definition of the term "scientific."

[2] For those wishing to pursue this topic in greater depth, please see C. Stephen Evans, *Preserving the Person: A Look at the Human Sciences* (Downers Grove, Ill.: InterVarsity, 1977); R. Hooykaas, *Religion and the Rise of Modern Science* (Grand Rapids: Eerdmans, 1972); Michael Polanyi, *Science, Faith and Society* (Chicago: University of Chicago Press, 1959); and Alan Storkey, *A Christian Social Perspective* (Leicester, U.K.: InterVarsity, 1979).

[3] One thinks, of course, of the political, economic, and social thought of the early Greeks in this regard, but it is also clear that the literature pertaining to many of the world's great religions contains a good deal of studied wisdom about the human condition. The writings of Confucius, though not essentially religious in objective, certainly assumed a highly developed understanding of human behavior as did the literature of the Hebrews and premodern Christians. We moderns, of course, would label much of this teaching as ethical in form (which it was) and thereby assume it to be qualitatively different from the social sciences of today. It *was* different, not because it taught an ethic, but because it did so explicitly.

[4] For an interesting discussion of the Christian influence in early American sociology, see David Lyon, "The Idea of a Christian Sociology," *Sociological Analysis*, vol. 44, no. 3 (Fall 1983): 227–42.

[5] My dissertation, along with those published articles based on it ("Religious Participation, Socioeconomic Status, and Belief-Orthodoxy," *Journal for the Scientific Study of Religion* [September 1977]; and "A Causal Model of Belief-Orthodoxy: Proposal and Empirical Test," *Sociological Analysis*, vol. 37, no. 3 [1976]), were essentially the products of objective science, based upon naturalistic assumptions.

⁶For example, see Meredith McGuire's otherwise outstanding text, *Religion: The Social Context* (Belmont, Calif.: Wadsworth, 1981), 2.

⁷The point here is not that the religious convert's interpretation of his or her own experience is necessarily correct (certainly it may not be), but that the objective scientist's interpretation is not neutral and ignores evidence that fails to fit into naturalistic categories.

⁸From this statement, one might conclude (erroneously, in my opinion) that the proper Christian approach to science is one which simply assumes that God works through the natural processes which objective science investigates. This would allow the Christian scientist to function as an objective scientist as long as he keeps God's sovereignty in the back of his mind.

The problem with this approach, however, is that it tends to be dualistic and is, at times, nothing more than an excuse to engage in naturalistic science. The reason, of course, is that this is after-the-fact integration; it provides a Christian explanation for an objective science conclusion. It does nothing to change one's approach to science, nor does it bring Christian assumptions to bear on the entire scientific enterprise. As a result, the Christian is still allowing a naturalistic world view to set the parameters for scientific thinking and doing.

For a general discussion of the issue, please see Robert A. Clark and S. D. Gaede, "Where Your Treasure Is: A Christian Exploration of the Sociology of Knowledge" (Paper delivered at the annual meeting of Association of Christians Teaching Sociology, Calvin College, June 1981).

⁹August Comte, *A General View of Positivism* (1848) (New York: Speller, 1957).

¹⁰They are not mutually exclusive because one may employ two or more of them at the same time; they are not exhaustive because there may be other "ways of knowing" (e.g. narrative, intuitive, etc.).

¹¹See *From Max Weber: Essays in Sociology*, trans. and ed. Han Gerth and C. Wright Mills (New York: Oxford University Press, 1946); note especially chapters 6 through 9.

¹²Karl Marx, *Capital: A Critique of Political Economy* (1867), ed. Friedrich Engels (New York: New World, 1967).

¹³Herbert Spencer's most influential work was probably *The Study of Sociology* (New York: Appleton, 1891); see also *First Principles* (New York: Appleton, 1898), and *An Autobiography*, 2 vols. (New York: Appleton, 1904).

¹⁴Aside from *Capital*, important works by Karl Marx would include *The Economic and Philosophical Manuscripts of 1844* (New York: International Publishers, 1964); *The Communist Manifesto* (1848), with Friedrich Engels (New York: Appleton, 1964); see also *Selected Writings in Sociology and Social Philosophy*, trans. T. B. Bottomore (London: McGraw-Hill, 1964).

Part B

[1] This does not mean, of course, that the social scientist is forever locked into a specific set of world view assumptions. People change—they modify their ultimate loyalties for good or ill—and scientists are people. Things happen to the social scientist, both within and outside of his research, which drive him to reformulate his understanding of the ultimate nature of reality. But whatever that understanding may be, it ought to be carefully thought through and consistently employed by the social scientist in question.

Chapter 7

[1] Gen. 1:1. All biblical quotes are taken from the *Revised Standard Version*.
[2] Gen. 1:28; 2:15–17.
[3] Gen. 2:18.
[4] Gen. 1:27.
[5] Gen. 3:9.
[6] Gen. 3:8.
[7] Gen. 3:8–24.
[8] Gen. 3:11.
[9] Gen. 3:16.
[10] Gen. 3:17–19.

Chapter 8

[1] By "consumerism," I mean the attempt to make consumption of material goods the primary source of personal fulfillment; it takes the God-given ability and need to consume and transforms it into an "end" or god (i.e., an "ism"). At times, consumerism has also been used to refer to the movement aimed at protecting the public from defective products, misleading advertising, and unethical business practices; obviously, that it not what I mean by the term (nor, for what it is worth, do I think it is an adequate description of a group trying to protect the consumer).

[2] J. A. Walters in *Sacred Cows* (Grand Rapids: Zondervan, 1979), provides a superb analysis of the social ramifications of what I have called creational idolatry, particularly in the West. Walter's work is a good example of a social science enlivened and informed by the assumptions of the Christian faith.

[3] A great deal of literature, of course, *is* produced on the topic of self-assurance and self-reliance—on how to attain it, not on how to avoid its problematics. Much of this is shot through with creational idolatry and much is written, unfortunately, by Christians. That such

material is gobbled up by Christian readers is clear evidence of the materialistic inclinations of the Western church.

⁴Please do not misunderstand this point. I am not opposed to romance; indeed, I think it is wonderful—a gift from God. But romantic love cannot replace our need for God and it ought not to be our ultimate source of security.

⁵Jacques Ellul has provided great enlightenment on this issue in *The Political Illusion* (New York: Vintage, 1972), and *False Presence of the Kingdom* (New York: Seabury, 1972). The reader unfamiliar with Ellul's works should begin with *The Presence of the Kingdom* (New York: Seabury, 1967), after which I recommend *The Technological Society* (New York: Vintage, 1964) and *The Meaning of the City*, trans. Dennis Pardee (Grand Rapids: Eerdmans, 1970). Ellul can be difficult and he is always frustrating. At points, I think he is quite wrong; but he is always provocative and clearly one of the great Christian social critics of our age.

Chapter 9

¹One gets a feeling for the importance of the "nature" metaphor by watching television specials on science, the universe, or its inhabitants. Over and over again, "nature" is employed as the reason for, or cause of, an event; it is the overseer, the one who keeps things in balance. This anthropomorphism, moreover, is presented without embarrassment as objective science.

²The reader seeking an anthropological overview of religion in non-Western societies may choose from among a number of modern texts, e.g., Anthony Wallace, *Religion: An Anthropological View* (New York: Random House, 1966), but I would suggest an old classic by Sir James Frazer: *The Golden Bough: A Study of Magic and Religion*, abridged edition (New York: Macmillan, 1922).

³The most obvious example is the Hindu doctrine of reincarnation, which assumes that the soul reappears after death in a different, not necessarily human, bodily form. While such an approach leads to a certain amount of needed respect for the animal kingdom, it can also contribute to human misery if animals are given the same existential rights as human beings. For the reader desiring an uncritical discussion of reincarnation, please see the chapter on Hinduism in Huston Smith, *The Religions of Man* (New York: Harper and Row, 1965).

⁴This error is especially evident in modern liberal theology, reaching its zenith in the "death of God" lurch, popularized by Thomas J. J. Altizer and William Hamilton, *Radical Theology and the Death of God* (Indianapolis: Bobbs-Merrill, 1966), ruminated on by John A. T. Robinson, *Honest to God* (Philadelphia: Westminster, 1963),

reveled in by Harvey Cox, *The Secular City* (New York: Macmillan, 1967), but rooted in the theological works of such as Rudolf Bultmann, *Theology of the New Testament*, vol. 1 (New York: Scribner, 1951), and *Theology of the New Testament*, vol. 2 (New York: Scribner, 1955); and Paul Tillich, *Systematic Theology*, vol. 1 (Chicago: University of Chicago Press, 1951), and *The Courage to Be* (New Haven: Yale University Press, 1952). One might say, however, that all of the above were attempting to come to terms with the thoughts of Nietzsche and Feuerbach within a Christian context.

[5] This tendency, on the other hand, is often found in the evangelical wing of the church. Here Jesus is viewed as such a "good old friend" that the believer can lose all sense of God's judgment or hatred of sin. This leads to an overemphasis on belief ("easy-believism") and a somewhat cavalier attitude toward the works which are to be the fruit of faith. Christ apparently did not have such an attitude (see Matt. 25:31–46), nor, for that matter, did the initiators of the American evangelical movement. See David Moberg, *The Great Reversal: Evangelism Versus Social Concern* (Philadelphia: Lippincott, 1972).

[6] This might have something to do with the inability of liberal Protestant theologians, even in their heyday, to appeal to the laity in their denominations. See Jeffrey K. Hadden, *The Gathering Storm in the Churches: The Widening Gap Between Clergy and Layman* (Garden City, N.Y.: Doubleday, 1969).

[7] No reason at all. I might add that I am indebted to Peter Berger for this insight, though he arrives at his conclusion from a somewhat different starting point. See Peter Berger, *The Sacred Canopy: Elements of a Sociological Theory of Religion* (Garden City, N.Y.: Doubleday, 1967): 155–71, and *A Rumor of Angels: Modern Society and the Rediscovery of the Supernatural* (Garden City, N.Y.: Doubleday, 1969), 19–27.

[8] Thomas O'Dea, in *The Sociology of Religion* (Englewood Cliffs, N.J.: Prentice-Hall, 1966), 7–19, offers a clear interpretation of the functional distinction between religion and magic.

[9] Erving Goffman, *Asylums* (Garden City, N.Y.: Doubleday, 1961).

Chapter 10

[1] This was not, however, the central assumption of humanism during the Middle Ages and Renaissance, at which time it referred to the study of classical literature and culture and was supported by numerous Christians. While a few modern Christians like to call themselves Christian humanists, the term has almost universally come to refer to a nontheistic view of human fulfillment. Obviously, I am using it in its modern sense.

²Aspects of denial, for example, seem to be involved in the events of the Flood (Gen. 6–8), the tower of Babel (Gen. 11:1–9), and Sodom and Gomorrah (Gen. 18–19).

³I am thinking not only of John Locke's work, *The Reasonableness of Christianity* (1695), but also the later efforts of some, such as Friedrich Schleiermacher, to understand the essence of religion through the study of human experiences of the infinite.

⁴Jean-Paul Sartre, *Being and Nothingness* (New York: Citadel, 1965), and *Nausea* (Norfolk, Conn.: New Directions, 1949).

⁵One sees this, for example, in the historical development of the sociology of knowledge literature. The materialists, such as Marx (see *Karl Marx: Selected Writings in Sociology and Social Philosophy*, ed. T. B. Bottomore [New York: McGraw-Hill, 1956]), stress the dependence of ideas on social conditions, while the idealists, such as Max Scheler in *Problems of a Sociology of Knowledge* (trans. Frings, ed. Stikkers [London: Routledge and Kegan Paul, 1980]), argue that values and ideals can transcend history and society. Few modern sociologists side with idealists.

⁶I know that in making this statement, I am getting beyond my turf. But, in some cases, the sovereignty-of-God-versus-free-will debate is nothing more than a theological version of the humanist-fatalist dilemma. Free-will advocates who really believe in "free" will are employing a humanist assumption. Sovereignty advocates who believe human choices are less than genuine—mere consequences of actions of the Great Puppeteer (*none* of the great Reformers believed this, I might add)—are playing the fatalist. There is room, of course, for theological articulation of the meaning of human choice and God's sovereignty. But that discussion ought not to exclude biblical truths for the sake of human finitude.

⁷This will not be easy to accomplish. Contemporary social science generally operates in either a determinist or choicist mode, the former during theoretical analysis and the latter when applying the analysis to a particular social problem (i.e., policy recommendations). This is one more reason why a biblical framework is imperative for the Christian social scientist.

⁸See Emile Durkheim, *The Elementary Forms of the Religious Life*, trans. Joseph W. Swain (1915; reprint, New York: Free Press, 1965), and Max Weber, *The Sociology of Religion*, trans. E. Fischoff (Boston: Beacon, 1963).

⁹For a discussion of the issues and debates surrounding the topic of secularization, see David Martin, *A General Theory of Secularization* (New York: Harper and Row, 1978).

¹⁰Rodney Stark and William S. Bainbridge, for example, argue that "secular societies" are ideal breeding grounds for new religious

movements ("Secularization and Cult Formations," *Journal for the Scientific Study of Religion* 20 [December 1981]: 360–72. Benton Johnson, "Church and Sect Revisited," *Journal for the Scientific Study of Religion* 10 (Summer 1971): 124–37 has noted, moreover, that sect movements can have a profound affect upon their host society. If these authors are correct, secularization is a far from an inexorable force.

[11]In the language of Peter Berger, this condition leads to alienation (*The Sacred Canopy: Elements of a Sociological Theory of Religion* [Garden City, N.Y.: Doubleday, 1967]: 81–101). This fusion of culture and transcendence, though evident at points in Christian history, is especially evident in Islamic societies.

Chapter 11

[1]This may appear to be a slam at capitalism, but such is not my intent. A free market can operate within a community where norms of justice, neighborly concern, and care for the poor operate. In such a community, maximizing consumption and/or profit will not be taken as an incontrovertible good, nor will individualism be the modus operandi. For a good discussion of the broader issue of justice and economic development, see Nicholas Wolterstorff, *Until Justice and Peace Embrace* (Grand Rapids: Eerdmans, 1983).

[2]Such an approach to Christianity couches a truth within a larger lie. The truth—that we must come before the Lord alone—is used to suggest that we ought to stay there, keeping our faith to ourselves. But, of course, the Christian faith is precisely an other-directed faith, forcing converts to reach out to their neighbors, community, nation, and the "uttermost parts of the earth."

The modern desire for a "private religion" has nothing to do with the nature of the Christian faith and everything to do with the nature of modern, pluralistic societies. For a general discussion of the latter, see Thomas Luckmann, *The Invisible Religion: The Problem of Religion in Modern Society* (New York: Macmillan, 1967). James Hunter discusses this issue in relation to the contemporary evangelical community in *American Evangelicalism: Conservative Religion and the Quandry of Modernity* (New Brunswick: Rutgers University Press, 1983).

[3]This is not to imply the reverse—that less freedom is better. That would simply employ the opposite form of denial, communalism. Neither freedom from others, nor communalistic fusion is the Christian ideal. Both are relational perversions.

[4]I am indebted to Alan Storkey's elaboration of this relationship. See *A Christian Social Perspective*, 41–44. For a general discussion of the social and political thought of Karl Marx, see Raymond Aaron, *Main Currents of Sociological Thought*, vol. 1 (New York: Basic Books, 1965).

[5] This is especially evident in Phillip Slater's work, *The Pursuit of Loneliness* (Boston: Beacon, 1976).

[6] Ferdinand Toennies, *Community and Society*, trans. Charles Loomis (East Lansing: Michigan State University Press, 1957).

[7] See Robert Redfield, "The Folk Society and Culture," *American Journal of Sociology*, vol. 45 (1940): 731–42; David Riesman, *The Lonely Crowd*, with Glazer and Denney (New Haven: Yale University Press, 1961); Emile Durkheim, *The Division of Labor in Society*, trans. G. Simpson (1893; reprint, New York: Free Press, 1960); and Max Weber, *The Theory of Social and Economic Organization*, trans. Henderson and Parsons, ed. Parsons (New York: Oxford University Press, 1947).

[8] Berger, *The Sacred Canopy: Elements of a Sociological Theory of Religion* (Garden City, N.Y.: Doubleday, 1967): 49, 50; 81–101.

[9] Though Talcott Parsons, *The Social System* (New York: Free Press, 1951), is given major credit (and abuse) for the development of functionalist theory, numerous influential sociologists and anthropologists have employed a functionalist perspective, including Robert Merton, *Social Theory and Social Structure* (New York: Free Press, 1964); Kingsley Davis and Wilbert E. Moore, "Some Principles of Stratification," *American Sociological Review* (April 1945): 242–49; and A. R. Radcliffe-Brown, "On the Concept of Function in Social Science," *American Anthropologist* 37 (1935): 395, 396.

[10] Though many conflict theorists find their inspiration in the thoughts of Karl Marx, they are not a homogeneous group; some of the best known are C. Wright Mills, *The Power Elite* (New York: Oxford University Press, 1956); Lewis Coser, *The Functions of Conflict* (New York: Free Press, 1956); Alvin Gouldner, *The Coming Crisis of Western Sociology* (New York: Avon, 1970); and Ralf Dahrendorf, *Class and Class Conflict in Industrial Society* (Stanford: Stanford University Press, 1959).

[11] This is a controversial conclusion because Toennies himself, in the preface to the final edition of *Gemeinschaft und Gesellschaft*, disclaimed any ethical or political intent in writing this book. Such a claim, however, must be viewed in terms of the desire of the author (1) to have his work read as a scientific treatise and (2) to disassociate himself from some of the political controversies within his nation (Germany, 1935). To gain scientific legitimacy, he had to claim a value-free perspective; to distance himself from the highly politicized notion of "community," he had to disclaim any personal interest in the subject. For a good discussion of Toennies's work, see Robert Nisbet, *The Sociological Tradition* (New York: Basic Books, 1966); note especially chapter 3, and pages 71–82.

[12] If I understand him correctly, however, Berger believes that they are only inevitable from the perspective of an objective scientist (what I would call a naturalistic scientist). From a humanistic perspective, he

thinks they are not inevitable. This interpretation is based upon his view of the scientific task as presented in his *Invitation to Sociology: A Humanistic Perspective* (Garden City, N.Y.: Doubleday, 1963) and in Peter Berger and Hansfried Kellner, *Sociology Reinterpreted: An Essay on Method and Vocation* (Garden City, N.Y.: Doubleday, 1981).

Chapter 12

[1]See J. A. Walters in *Sacred Cows* (Grand Rapids: Zondervan, 1979), 25–46, for an insightful discussion of the Western approach to work.

[2]The familiar notion of property as an "inalienable right" comes very close to a technologist perspective on the environment. For a description of the non-Christian origins, development, and consequences of the concept, see Alan Storkey, *A Christian Social Perspective* (Leicester, U.K.: InterVarsity, 1979), 320–34.

[3]This may help to explain why, in their contact with Western technology, some cultures put up with it reluctantly (see Margaret Mead, *The Changing Culture of an Indian Tribe* [New York: Columbia University Press, 1932]), while others imitate it with abandon (see Peter Worsley, *The Trumpet Shall Sound: A Study of Cargo Cults in Melanesia* [New York: Schocken Books, 1968]).

[4]Jacques Ellul paints a vivid picture of the power behind the forces of technique in *The Technological Society* and *The Meaning of the City*.

[5]Alvin Toffler, *Future Shock* (New York: Random House, 1970); the notion of "cultural lag" was developed originally by Charles Ogburn, *Social Change* (New York: Viking, 1950).